Anissa Brodon

Decluttering for Empty Nesters

52 Weeks of Letting Go (and Laughing Along the Way)

Anissa Brodon

Welcome to the Empty Nest
(and the Full Cupboard)

So… the kids are out of the house.

The bedrooms are suspiciously quiet.

The fridge no longer mysteriously empties itself overnight.

And for the first time in *possibly ever*, your laundry basket has space in it.

Congratulations! You've officially earned your "Empty Nester" badge.

But as you settle into this next phase of life—one that hopefully involves more sleep, less driving, and the occasional hot cup of tea that doesn't go cold—you might start noticing something else that's been left behind: **stuff**. So. Much. Stuff. Tiny socks. Broken crayons. 4,298 pieces of glitter. Six phone chargers, none of which fit your phone. And that's just what's in one drawer.

Welcome to the bittersweet side of parenting's finish line: **clutter with feelings**. You're not just dealing with boxes and bags—you're navigating a minefield of memories. Every drawer is a time capsule. Every closet door you open whispers, "Remember when they were five?" And every mug says "#1 Mom," even if it's chipped and hasn't been used since the early 2000s.

This book is your permission slip to laugh, cry, sort, toss, and keep what really matters. It's not about minimalism for the sake of it. It's about **making space for the life you're living now**, while honoring the beautiful, messy one you've already lived. Over the next 52 weeks, we'll tackle clutter zone by zone—one junk drawer, forgotten shelf, and mystery box at a time. You'll get stories, step-by-step tips, and a weekly checklist that's more satisfying than watching your kids finally do their own laundry.

No pressure. No guilt. Just a year of reclaiming your space, your time, and maybe even your sanity. You've earned this. Let's go find your floor.

Week 1: The Sock Drawer of Doom

There's a drawer in every household that defies the laws of time and space. Ours was the sock drawer. It started as an innocent little tray with neatly rolled pairs. Over the years, it morphed into a textile abyss—a Bermuda Triangle of foot fashion. Opening it required courage, a flashlight, and occasionally, a tetanus shot.

I once found a baby sock in there. My youngest is now 27. Another time, I pulled out a single glittery unicorn sock, which I'm pretty sure belonged to a neighbor's kid. Where do the matching socks go? Is there a secret sock society living behind the dryer? These are questions we may never answer. But today, we make peace with the drawer—and with the memories stuffed in it.

🎯 The Weekly Declutter Focus

Target Zone: Your primary sock drawer (and bonus points if you hit any overflow sock baskets, laundry room orphans, or rogue sock piles under beds).
Goal: Find the pairs you actually wear, retire the ones you don't, and free up space for joy—not mystery lint.

🗑 Letting Go Tip + Memory Keeper Tip

Letting Go Tip: If a sock doesn't have a match, hasn't been worn in over a year, or is somehow more hole than fabric—it's time. Your feet deserve better.

Memory Keeper Tip: If there's a baby sock or a silly pair with sentimental value, keep **one**. Place it in a memory box or shadow frame. It doesn't have to take up the whole drawer to still hold meaning.

👜 Organising Advice

Once you've culled the herd, sort your socks by type: everyday, fancy, fuzzy, sport, and seasonal. Store them rolled or folded—whatever makes you smile when you open the drawer. Use little drawer dividers if you're feeling fancy. Label sections if you want to feel like the CEO of Sock World.

Hot tip: Keep a "lonely sock" bag in the laundry room. Reunions happen.

💪 Mini Motivational Boost

This isn't just a drawer—it's a symbol. A sign that you're finally reclaiming space. You are no longer the Keeper of Everyone's Socks. You are the Queen (or King) of Your Drawer Kingdom. Celebrate the small victories—especially if you can now open and close the drawer without causing a textile avalanche.

Checklist for the Week

- Empty the sock drawer completely
- Match all socks and lay them out
- Toss stained, holey, or stretched-out pairs
- Recycle lonely socks (cleaning rags!) or discard
- Keep only what fits, feels good, and gets worn
- Organize by type or color
- Place one sentimental sock aside if needed
- Take a drawer victory photo (for you, not Instagram—unless you're into that)

"One to Keep, One to Toss" Challenge

Keep: That one ridiculous pair you wear every Christmas and secretly love.
Toss: The saggy pair you've been pretending are "bed socks," but which feel like wearing two wet paper towels.

Week 2: Junk Drawer Jenga

There was a time when I believed the junk drawer was a temporary solution. A transitional space. A quick-fix landing pad for things on their way to somewhere else. That was about 20 years ago. Since then, it's evolved into a catch-all jungle of birthday candles, dried-up pens, batteries of questionable origin, and a mystery key that might open a gate in Narnia.

I once reached in for a pen and pulled out a rogue marble, two twisty ties, and a baby tooth (unlabeled—hopefully human). The worst part? I still didn't find a working pen. But this week, we finally face the drawer, armed with a trash bag, a sense of humor, and a firm "no" to expired coupons from 2006.

◎ The Weekly Declutter Focus

Target Zone: The infamous junk drawer (you know the one).
Goal: Sort the usable from the baffling, and create a drawer that functions like a helpful tool—not a chaotic time capsule.

🗑 Letting Go Tip + Memory Keeper Tip

Letting Go Tip: Be ruthless. If you don't know what it is, or it's broken, dried out, or belongs to a device you haven't seen since 2011, out it goes. The drawer should serve you—not confuse you.

Memory Keeper Tip: If you find a sweet old note from your kid, a tiny doodle, or a memento with meaning, give it a proper home. Tape it inside your journal or add it to a memory box—not the same clutter pit where you store loose screws and dead batteries.

🧺 Organising Advice

Dump the entire drawer on a surface (brace yourself). Group similar items: tools, tape, pens, batteries, keys, coins, etc. Create simple zones with drawer dividers, mini trays, or even old jar lids. If it doesn't belong in a junk drawer (like buttons, hair ties, or Lego pieces), rehome it. Think: helpful, not hoarder.

Pro tip: Keep a tiny notepad or pen stash here too —functional AND fancy.

💪 Mini Motivational Boost

Cleaning your junk drawer is a declaration of control. You are no longer ruled by rogue birthday candles and bent paper clips. You're creating a drawer with purpose—and maybe even a pen that writes. That, my friend, is transformation.

Checklist for the Week

Decluttering for Empty Nesters

- Empty the drawer fully and clean it out
- Toss the junk: broken, expired, unidentifiable
- Sort and group remaining items by type
- Rehome anything that doesn't belong here
- Use dividers or small containers to organize
- Keep it useful: scissors, tape, batteries, pens
- Place a sticky note inside with the date you cleaned it—future you will be proud
- Do a dramatic "drawer close" with a flourish

One to Keep, One to Toss Challenge

Keep: The mini screwdriver you always reach for.
Toss: The rubber band so old it disintegrates when touched.

Week 3: Tupperware—The Plastic Bermuda Triangle

It starts innocently enough. A few containers for leftovers. A matching set, if you're lucky. But give it a few years, a few birthdays, and a few "I'll just keep this one from the takeaway" moments, and suddenly you're the proud owner of 47 containers—and 13 lids. None of which fit.

I once opened the cupboard and got smacked in the face by a rogue sandwich box. Not aggressively, but with just enough force to say, "You've lost control of this situation." I even found a lid labeled with my child's name written in crayon. He moved out six years ago. Clearly, it's time to face the plastics. With courage. And a bin.

🎯 The Weekly Declutter Focus

Target Zone: Food storage containers—Tupperware, takeaway tubs, mismatched lids, all of it. **Goal:** Match, stack, and simplify. Keep what you use, ditch what you dread.

🗑 Letting Go Tip + Memory Keeper Tip

Letting Go Tip: If it's warped, cracked, stained beyond saving, or lidless, it's not your problem anymore. You are not a storage archaeologist. You are a grown adult who deserves a lid that fits the first time.

Memory Keeper Tip: If there's a container tied to a beloved memory (lunches packed for first days of school, cookies baked for science fairs), clean it up and repurpose it as a keepsake box for letters or trinkets.

🧺 Organising Advice

Pull out all your containers. Match lids to bases like it's a high-stakes dating show. Anything without a partner gets recycled or tossed. Stack by size to save space. Store lids upright in a bin or tray—never loose. If you're constantly battling avalanche shelves, consider switching to stackable glass or uniform sets. Life-changing.

Bonus move: Keep one or two containers just for gifting leftovers. That way, when someone "forgets" to return it, you don't need therapy.

💪 Mini Motivational Boost

This is more than tidying plastic. This is reclaiming a cupboard—and your sanity. No more lid roulette. No more storing spaghetti in that one bowl you secretly hate. This is a leap toward a more peaceful kitchen (and forehead).

Checklist for the Week

- Remove all containers and lids from cupboards/drawers
- Match every lid to a base
- Toss/recycle damaged or lidless items
- Keep only what you regularly use and love
- Stack containers by size/type
- Store lids vertically for easy access
- Clean the cupboard/drawer before putting items back
- Do a happy little dance when nothing falls on you

One to Keep, One to Toss Challenge

Keep: The perfectly sized container you use every week.

Toss: The lid with no partner and no hope—may it rest in pieces.

Week 4: Where Old Chargers Go to Die

At some point, our home became a retirement village for obsolete electronics. Chargers for phones that haven't worked since MySpace was popular. USB cables that don't fit anything. A mystery tangle of cords so knotted, I considered calling in a priest. I found a power brick the size of a small loaf of bread—no idea what it once powered, but I'm convinced it's been humming threateningly for years.

And here's the kicker: we keep them *just in case.* In case what? Time travel? The return of the flip phone? This week, we face the cords, the tech relics, the awkward adapters—and we reclaim not just a drawer or a box, but a little peace of mind.

🎯 The Weekly Declutter Focus

Target Zone: All drawers, bins, and baskets hoarding old chargers, cables, batteries, headphones, and tech accessories.
Goal: Eliminate what's outdated or unidentifiable and neatly organize the cords and accessories you actually use.

🗑 Letting Go Tip + Memory Keeper Tip

Letting Go Tip: If you can't name what it's for, toss it. If the device it charged no longer exists (or works), let it go. And if it's frayed, sparking, or smells like regret—it's not worth the fire hazard.

Memory Keeper Tip: If there's a nostalgic device you can't part with—like an old iPod or flip phone—keep *one* as a memory piece in a labeled "Tech Time Capsule" box. Not your bedside drawer.

🧺 Organising Advice

Gather every cord and charger from around the house. Match them to their devices if possible (label as you go—masking tape and a pen are your best friends). For keepers, use cord ties or small zip bags to avoid future chaos. Store all active-use tech in one central drawer or box. Create a separate box labeled "spare cords" and revisit in six months to toss what's still untouched.

Want to get fancy? Use a label maker. Want to feel amazing? Don't.

Mini Motivational Boost

This is a big one. Tech clutter creates sneaky stress —it's ugly, tangled, and frustrating when you're in a hurry. By clearing it out, you're saying "no" to digital dead weight and "yes" to a home that works for *today's* life—not tech ghosts of Christmas past.

Checklist for the Week

o Collect all cords, chargers, batteries, tech bits from every room
o Match chargers with devices (label them if you're feeling bold)
o Toss frayed, broken, or mystery cords
o Recycle old tech responsibly (many stores offer drop-offs)
o Store cords in bags, ties, or labeled containers
o Create one small box for "spares" and mark a revisit date
o Wipe out drawers or bins you emptied
o Breathe deeply. You have tamed the Cable Kraken

One to Keep, One to Toss Challenge

Keep: The charger you actually use every single day.
Toss: The adapter for a 2004 camera you haven't seen since the Spice Girls' last reunion.

Week 5: Linen Closet of Forgotten Towels

Once upon a time, I had a system. Bath towels on one shelf, guest towels neatly folded, hand towels rolled up like a spa ad. Fast forward a few years—and several "I'll just stuff it in for now" moments—and the linen closet became a textile avalanche waiting to happen. I opened the door one morning and a pink beach towel from 2008 lunged at me in protest.

Some of the towels are so old, they've developed what I call "perma-damp"—that funky, never-quite-dry scent of regret. Others are just... stiff. Like they've been through one too many emotional dryer cycles. But this week, we tackle the closet. We fold with purpose. We sort like heroes. And we finally figure out where that Winnie the Pooh washcloth came from.

◎ The Weekly Declutter Focus

Target Zone: Linen closet or linen shelf—wherever your towels, sheets, and washcloths live (or hide).
Goal: Keep only what's useful, fresh, and loved. Clear out the stiff, the sad, and the surplus.

🗑 Letting Go Tip + Memory Keeper Tip

Letting Go Tip: If it's threadbare, stained, crunchy, or smells like a gym locker after a rainstorm—let it go. Your skin deserves better.

Memory Keeper Tip: If you have a towel or baby blanket with deep sentimental value, fold it gently into your memory box or turn it into a keepsake pillow. Don't let it rot in a pile of hand towels.

🧺 Organising Advice

Take everything out—yes, all of it. Sort towels into categories: bath, hand, face, guest, beach, sentimental. Fold what you love and actually use. Roll extras to save space or stack by size. Donate usable extras to animal shelters—they always need towels. Label shelf zones if you want to feel wildly accomplished.

And for the love of fluff—stop saving more than two "just in case" towels. You are not running a B&B.

💪 Mini Motivational Boost

Your linen closet shouldn't be a place of fear. It should be a haven of fluffy joy. Today, you're not just folding fabric—you're crafting comfort. And eliminating the low-key stress that comes with digging through a mess when you just need a decent towel.

Checklist for the Week

- Empty the linen closet completely
- Sort into: keep, donate, toss, memory
- Check all linens for wear, stains, and weird smells
- Fold neatly by type (or roll for space-saving flair)
- Store like with like—towels, sheets, etc.
- Donate clean extras to local shelters
- Wipe down and air out the shelves
- Close the door and sigh with pride instead of dread

🎁 One to Keep, One to Toss Challenge

Keep: Your coziest towel that feels like a hug from a cloud.
Toss: The scratchy beach towel with the weird bleach stain and no known origin.

Week 6: The Attack of the Expired Spices

There comes a moment in every home cook's life when they reach for the cinnamon... and realize it expired during the Obama administration. I once found a jar of nutmeg so ancient, I'm fairly certain it could have seasoned the first Thanksgiving. Some of these spices are so old, they've turned into tiny scented rocks—great for doorstops, not so much for dinner.

And let's not even talk about the duplicates. Why did I own three full jars of paprika? Was I planning to open a paprika-only restaurant? Probably not. This week, it's time to take back the spice shelf. Say goodbye to the crumpled packets, crusty lids, and questionable curry powders. Your taste buds will thank you.

🎯 The Weekly Declutter Focus

Target Zone: Spice rack, spice cupboard, pantry spices, and any rogue jars hiding behind the olive oil.
Goal: Toss the expired, consolidate the duplicates, and create a spice zone that sparks joy (or at least smells nice).

🗑️ Letting Go Tip + Memory Keeper Tip

Letting Go Tip: If it's expired, smells like dust, or has turned into a single clump of mysterious origin, it's got to go. You deserve spices that spice.

Memory Keeper Tip: If there's a spice tied to a memory—maybe a jar you used every holiday—snap a photo of it and write the recipe down. Let the memory live on, not the moldy oregano.

🧺 Organising Advice

Pull out all the spices and line them up. Check expiration dates. Smell-test anything suspicious. Group by type: baking, savory, hot, sweet. Keep them in clear view—alphabetized if you're fancy, basketed if you're practical. Label the tops or use a lazy Susan if shelf space is tight.

Avoid spice hoarding unless you *actually* use turmeric in three meals a week.

Mini Motivational Boost

Decluttering your spice stash is a little act of self-care that pays off every time you cook. No more "Is this cumin or mystery dust?" moments. Just smooth, joyful cooking and a sense of smug adulting every time you open the cupboard.

✅ Checklist for the Week

o Take out every spice jar, bottle, and packet

- o Check expiration dates and toss anything expired
- o Smell-test anything questionable
- o Group by type or frequency of use
- o Combine duplicates if still fresh
- o Clean sticky jars and wipe down the shelf
- o Label tops or containers if needed
- o Re-stock neatly and vow to check them once a year (or decade)

🗑 One to Keep, One to Toss Challenge

Keep: Your favorite, always-used spice that still smells amazing.
Toss: The crusty jar of dried basil that looks like green sawdust and expired five apartments ago.

Week 7: The "Just in Case" Cupboard (a.k.a. Doomsday Prep Lite)

We all have one. That shelf, basket, or cupboard full of items we might need one day—but haven't touched since 2012. A fondue pot, two dozen hotel sewing kits, a flashlight with no batteries, and a manual can opener (because what if the robots take over?). I once found six half-burned candles and a packet of yeast that expired in the same year my child started secondary school.

There's something oddly comforting about this zone. It makes us feel prepared. Equipped. Ready to survive a power outage, spontaneous craft session, or zombie apocalypse. But let's be honest: 90% of it is clutter hiding behind the mask of responsibility. This week, we ditch the false security and keep only what's truly useful. No, you don't need four rolls of neon duct tape. Not unless your hobby is kidnapping yourself.

🎯 The Weekly Declutter Focus

Target Zone: That cabinet, shelf, or box filled with "just in case" items—emergency gear, random tools, expired non-perishables, and miscellaneous back-ups.
Goal: Keep the truly useful emergency essentials and

toss the expired, absurd, and overly optimistic survival fantasies.

Letting Go Tip + Memory Keeper Tip

Letting Go Tip: If you haven't used it in the past 5+ years, can't remember what it does, or have 17 of them "just in case," it's probably not your survival item —it's clutter.

Memory Keeper Tip: Found something that once meant something (like that old emergency radio from your first home)? Snap a pic and write a quick caption in your memory journal. You don't need the bulk to keep the story.

Organising Advice

Sort items into three piles: *Actually Useful*, *Mildly Paranoid*, and *Why Did I Buy This?* Check dates on non-perishables, batteries, and meds. Group emergency supplies together—torch, radio, batteries, candles—in a labeled, accessible box. Store backup tools only if they're in working order. Donate duplicate kitchen gadgets or tools to local shelters or charity shops.

If your cupboard looks like you could survive six winters but barely host one dinner, scale back.

Mini Motivational Boost

There's bravery in releasing things you thought you might need. It means trusting that you'll handle life as it comes, rather than stockpiling for every possible storm. That's not recklessness—it's resilience. Plus, it frees up actual space for actual life.

Checklist for the Week

- Empty the "just in case" cupboard or shelf
- Sort into: useful, duplicate, broken, expired
- Test and group emergency gear
- Recycle or discard expired non-perishables
- Rehome or donate items you truly won't use
- Store essentials in a labeled, easy-to-reach container
- Wipe down and reorganize the space
- Give yourself a "prepared but not hoarding" gold star

🎁 One to Keep, One to Toss Challenge

Keep: A working flashlight and a few true emergency essentials.
Toss: That mystery gadget you bought at a petrol station in 2009 and still don't know how to use.

Week 8: Under the Bed—A Dust Bunny Safari

Ah yes, the land beneath the bed: where things go to hide, hibernate, and occasionally haunt. It's part storage space, part archaeological dig. I once found an empty chocolate wrapper, two mismatched socks, a birthday card from 2013, and a book I'd claimed was "borrowed by the cat." Not to mention enough dust to knit a sweater.

Under-bed storage starts as a good idea. "Seasonal clothes," we say. "Extra bedding." But over time, it becomes a black hole of forgotten fitness gear, mysterious cables, and the occasional haunted slipper. This week, grab a torch, a tissue, and maybe a brave friend—we're going in.

🎯 The Weekly Declutter Focus

Target Zone: Everything hiding under the bed—bins, boxes, loose items, dust colonies, and the occasional rogue shoe.
Goal: Clear it out, clean it up, and keep only what actually serves you.

🗑 Letting Go Tip + Memory Keeper Tip

Letting Go Tip: If it's under the bed and you haven't missed it in a year, chances are you don't need it. Be ruthless. You are not a squirrel. You don't need to stash "just in case" stuff beneath your sleeping zone.

Memory Keeper Tip: Found a love letter? A tiny stuffed animal? A sentimental shirt? If it sparks warm fuzzies, place it in your memory box—not under your mattress like a forgotten diary entry.

🧺 Organising Advice

Pull *everything* out from under the bed—yes, even the ominous stuff. Vacuum or sweep the whole area (prepare for dust tumbleweeds). Sort by category: keep, donate, toss. Use flat storage bins for things you truly want to keep (like off-season clothes or gift wrap). Label bins. And, ideally, keep the space minimal—less stuff = better sleep energy.

If it doesn't fit in a shallow, clearly labeled container, it doesn't belong there.

Mini Motivational Boost

Your bed should be a place of rest, not a hiding spot for forgotten baggage. Decluttering under it frees both physical space and mental energy. And let's be honest—there's something empowering about knowing *exactly* what's under there (and that it's not silently judging you).

Checklist for the Week

- Remove all items from under the bed
- Vacuum or sweep thoroughly
- Toss anything broken, outdated, or dusty beyond redemption
- Rehome items that don't belong in the bedroom
- Store keepers in flat, labeled storage bins
- Limit under-bed storage to essentials only
- Consider rotating seasonal items in or out
- Take a moment to lie down and appreciate the clear space beneath you

One to Keep, One to Toss Challenge

Keep: A storage bin with clearly labeled seasonal bedding.
Toss: That weird half-deflated exercise ball from your "motivated" phase.

Week 9: That One Drawer Full of Pens That Don't Work

It starts innocently. A pen here, a marker there. Before long, you've got a drawer full of writing instruments that *might* work—if the moon is full, you shake them hard enough, and whisper ancient incantations. I once found a quill. A literal feather quill. I've never owned an ink pot in my life.

And yet, there they sit. Dried-out biros, exploded gel pens, mystery highlighters, and that one fancy fountain pen you keep for "important letters" that never come. This week, we crack open the drawer, grab a notepad, and give every pen the test of truth. Spoiler: most will fail.

🎯 The Weekly Declutter Focus

Target Zone: Desk drawers, pen jars, catch-all containers filled with pens, markers, pencils, and writing tools.
Goal: Keep only the pens that actually write. Remove the dry, crusty, and mysterious from circulation.

🗑 Letting Go Tip + Memory Keeper Tip

Letting Go Tip: If you have to scribble like you're starting a fire just to make it write—it's done. Pens should not come with emotional labor.

Memory Keeper Tip: If a pen reminds you of something meaningful—like a graduation gift or one with your child's handwriting etched into it—set it aside in your keepsake box. Don't let it rot next to the exploded Sharpie.

Organising Advice

Grab a piece of scrap paper and test each pen. If it writes clearly and smoothly, it stays. If not, toss it. Keep a few of each kind: black pens, colored pens, a pencil or two, a marker. Use a mug, tray, or desk caddy to keep them tidy—and maybe label it, just to feel extra accomplished.

Consider designating one drawer or caddy as your "official writing center." Anything that doesn't earn a spot doesn't get to stay.

Mini Motivational Boost

There's something deeply satisfying about knowing every pen you pick up will *work*. No more angry scribbling. No more muttering under your breath. Just smooth lines, productive energy, and desk drawer peace.

Checklist for the Week

- Gather all pens, pencils, markers from around the house
- Test each one on scrap paper
- Toss any that don't write
- Wipe down your desk drawers and pen containers
- Sort and store pens by type or purpose
- Keep only the quantity you realistically use
- Create one easy-to-reach pen station
- Do a victory doodle with your favorite working pen

🎁 One to Keep, One to Toss Challenge

Keep: The pen that glides like a dream and makes you want to write thank-you notes.
Toss: The three identical hotel pens that gave up in 2011.

Week 10: The Kids' Art Pile That Might Be Worth Millions (Emotionally)

Ah yes, the priceless Picasso years—when every handprint, stick figure, and glitter explosion was declared "too special to ever throw away." And so you didn't. You saved every single one. The finger painting from nursery. The pasta owl. The inexplicable blob titled *My Dad Roaring Like a Bear*.

And now? You have a mountain of faded construction paper, half-unraveled macaroni necklaces, and mysterious scribbles that may—or may not—have been a family portrait. It's sentimental gold... and a fire hazard. This week, we face the pile with love and logic. Let's honor their creativity without drowning in decades of dried glue.

🎯 The Weekly Declutter Focus

Target Zone: Art drawers, bins, portfolios, folders, under-bed piles, and *that* kitchen drawer that's more collage than utility.
Goal: Curate a small, meaningful collection and release the rest (preferably without glitter explosions).

🗑 Letting Go Tip + Memory Keeper Tip

Letting Go Tip: Keep the standouts—the "wow" pieces, the milestones, the ones that still make you smile or cry. Let go of the endless piles of scribbles, practice sheets, and "I think this is a turkey?" guesses.

Memory Keeper Tip: Choose 10–15 of your favorites and store them in a flat, labeled memory box or art portfolio. You can also digitize the rest—scan or photograph them and create a digital gallery or photo book. That way, nothing gets lost, but your hallway won't look like an art studio exploded.

👜 Organising Advice

Sort the art into three piles: *Keep*, *Digitize*, and *Recycle with Tears.* Use a scanner or your phone to digitize anything you love but don't need in physical form. Consider creating one binder or accordion file per child with plastic sleeves for the highlights. Bonus: Let your now-grown kids help choose what to save. You might be surprised what they actually remember (or don't).

Whatever you do—label, date, and keep the glitter contained.

💪 Mini Motivational Boost

Letting go of your kids' artwork isn't letting go of them. You're just making space for *your* next masterpiece (and clearing a path to the back of the closet). Love what you keep. Bless what you release. And maybe keep the pasta owl. That thing is a legend.

Checklist for the Week

- Gather all kids' artwork from every drawer, box, and folder
- Create piles: Keep, Digitize, Recycle
- Choose standout pieces that tell a story or spark emotion
- Photograph or scan anything you want to preserve digitally
- Create one labeled memory box or folder per child
- Recycle or gently let go of faded, forgotten, or mystery pieces
- Wipe down and repurpose any newly cleared drawers or bins
- Maybe frame one epic piece just for fun

🎁 One to Keep, One to Toss Challenge

Keep: The painting they proudly signed and gifted to you.
Toss: The 47th abstract scribble titled "My Feelings (Maybe)."

Week 11: The Sentimental Shoe Graveyard

We all have them: the heels we wore once to a wedding in 2007, the running shoes from that "fitness era," the boots that look amazing but feel like foot prisons, and those ballet flats with holes you claim you *still* wear "around the house."

At some point, your shoe collection stops being functional and starts resembling an emotional timeline. "These were my interview shoes," "These were my first parent-teacher conference shoes," "These were the ones I wore the day the dog got loose and I had to sprint down the road." They're not just shoes—they're archives. But unless you're opening a Shoe Museum of Personal Triumphs, it's time to retire some of the old legends.

◎ The Weekly Declutter Focus

Target Zone: Closets, under-bed storage, shoe racks, hallway chaos zones—wherever shoes go to linger.
Goal: Keep only the shoes that fit, function, and make you feel fantastic.

🗑 Letting Go Tip + Memory Keeper Tip

Decluttering for Empty Nesters

Letting Go Tip: If they pinch, flop, squeak, or require band-aids every time you wear them—they're not serving you. Comfort and joy are non-negotiable. And if you haven't worn them in two years? You probably never will.

Memory Keeper Tip: Choose one sentimental pair to save—the wedding shoes, the tiny toddler boots, or the ones from your first "adult" job. Clean them, label them, and store them in a memory box, not your everyday closet.

🧺 Organising Advice

Pull out *every* pair. Yes, even the dusty ones in the garage. Try on anything you haven't worn in a while. Be honest about comfort and frequency of use. Sort into categories: daily wear, seasonal, special occasion, donate, and retire. Use shoe racks, clear boxes, or over-the-door organizers to make your favorites easy to grab.

Pro tip: Store shoes in pairs. Not "somewhere near each other in theory." This isn't a treasure hunt.

💪 Mini Motivational Boost

This isn't about giving up your style—it's about giving your feet the love they deserve. Every pair you keep should make you feel confident, comfortable, and just a little bit fabulous. Life's too short for shoes that betray you halfway through brunch.

Checklist for the Week

- Pull out all shoes from every corner of your home
- Try on questionable pairs and check for comfort and wear
- Toss or donate anything that doesn't fit or gets no use
- Sort keepers into categories: everyday, occasion, seasonal
- Wipe down or clean shoes before storing
- Organize by frequency of use or shoe type
- Store sentimental keepers in a memory box—not the main closet
- Celebrate with a walk in your comfiest pair

🎁 One to Keep, One to Toss Challenge

Keep: The pair that always makes you feel like you've got your life together.
Toss: The strappy sandals that require three bandages and a prayer to survive.

Week 12: The Coat Closet Black Hole

There's something magical about the coat closet. Not in the *Narnia* kind of way—more like *Hoarders: Outerwear Edition*. I once opened ours and had a scarf avalanche. Beneath it? A ski jacket from a trip we never took, a single glove with no known match, and three raincoats that have never actually seen rain.

Coat closets are where optimism and practicality go to wrestle. We keep coats "just in case" it snows in April, we're invited to a surprise ski weekend, or the kids *suddenly* grow back into that jacket from Year 8. Spoiler: They won't. This week, it's time to defrost the clutter and bring back breathable space.

🎯 The Weekly Declutter Focus

Target Zone: The hallway or entryway coat closet (or wherever coats, scarves, and seasonal gear go to breed).
Goal: Keep only current, useful, and comfortable outerwear. Retire what no longer fits your life—or your weather.

🗑️ Letting Go Tip + Memory Keeper Tip

Letting Go Tip: If it doesn't fit, hasn't been worn in two seasons, or is more "itchy regret" than "snuggly chic," it goes. You only need one emergency coat. Not eight.

Memory Keeper Tip: Is there a kid's coat or scarf with deep sentimental value? Keep one. Fold it gently into your memory box, or take a photo and let it go with gratitude.

🧺 Organising Advice

Pull *everything* out of the closet. Yes, everything. Try on coats for size and comfort (and to confirm that one isn't still stuffed with old tissues—spoiler: it is). Check pockets. Group items by category: daily wear, formal, winter accessories, guests. Use hooks or labeled bins for hats, gloves, and scarves. Add a small donation bag right inside the closet to keep it future-proof.

Pro tip: One jacket per person per season is usually more than enough.

Mini Motivational Boost

A tidy coat closet is like a warm hug when you're rushing out the door. You don't need a collection—you need confidence that whatever you grab actually fits, feels good, and doesn't smell like mothballs. Let yourself feel *light*, even when you're dressing for a snowstorm.

Checklist for the Week

- Empty the entire coat closet
- Sort coats, jackets, scarves, hats, and gloves
- Try on and check for fit, condition, and comfort
- Donate or toss anything you haven't worn in two+ years
- Wipe down shelves, vacuum the floor
- Use baskets or bins for accessories
- Hang only seasonally appropriate and wearable coats
- Add a "donate later" bin in the closet for future ease

One to Keep, One to Toss Challenge

Keep: The go-to coat that fits like a dream and goes with everything.
Toss: The jacket with the broken zipper you keep "just in case"—case closed.

Week 13: Pantry Purgatory—Expired Goods & Ghost Snacks

You know that moment when you reach for a snack… and pull out a granola bar that expired before your last child graduated? Welcome to Pantry Purgatory—the sacred storage zone where hope goes to expire. I once found a can of chickpeas that could've starred in a history documentary. Right beside it? Three open bags of rice cakes (all stale, all somehow *still* in the snack bin).

We all stash food with the best of intentions—healthy habits, backup meals, emergency rations—but somewhere along the way, it turns into a supermarket time capsule. This week, we dust off the shelves, face the stale, and finally get rid of that "experimental" quinoa mix no one ever touched.

◎ The Weekly Declutter Focus

Target Zone: Kitchen pantry, food cupboards, snack drawers, and any overflow snack baskets.
Goal: Keep only fresh, usable food. Discard the expired, donate the good-but-ignored, and rediscover your shelf space.

🗑 Letting Go Tip + Memory Keeper Tip

Letting Go Tip: If it's expired, opened and stale, or something no one in your house will eat (despite your hopeful delusions), it's time. Guilt doesn't make food taste better.

Memory Keeper Tip: If you find a nostalgic item—like a box of tea your grandma always drank—take a photo or save the label. Honor the memory without keeping expired groceries.

🧺 Organising Advice

Take *everything* out. Check expiration dates. Group similar items together—grains, snacks, canned goods, baking supplies. Donate non-expired but unused items to a food bank. Use bins or baskets to corral categories and label them. Keep the everyday items at eye level and the "occasionally used" items up high or down low.

Wipe every shelf before restocking—yes, even that sticky one.

💪 Mini Motivational Boost

Your pantry should work for you, not guilt-trip you. It's not a museum of failed diet plans or forgotten meal kits. By clearing it out, you're making room for real nourishment—and maybe even inspiration to cook something fun. At the very least, you'll stop knocking over expired breadcrumbs every time you reach for the pasta.

✅ Checklist for the Week

- Empty all shelves and drawers in the pantry area
- Check expiration dates—yes, even spices and condiments
- Toss anything stale, expired, or leaking regret
- Donate unused non-expired goods
- Wipe down shelves and sticky spots
- Group like with like and use bins to contain categories
- Label bins or shelves if it helps you keep it that way
- Do a happy pantry dance. You earned it.

One to Keep, One to Toss Challenge

Keep: The pantry staple you actually use and love (hello, pasta!).
Toss: That bag of kale chips that tasted like punishment and still haunts you.

Week 14: The Forgotten Luggage of Dreams

Ah, luggage. Once the symbol of adventure, spontaneity, and that magical thing called "holiday mode." Now? It's mostly stacked awkwardly on top of the wardrobe or stuffed in a cupboard, housing last summer's sand and a neck pillow that smells like 2014. I once opened a suitcase and found three flip-flops. Not three pairs—just three shoes. All different.

Luggage can hold memories… and also receipts, expired suncream, and every travel adapter you've ever owned (none of which work in the country you're going to next). This week, we unpack the dreams and the dust bunnies. Time to let go of what's broken, downsize the extras, and reclaim the space.

🎯 The Weekly Declutter Focus

Target Zone: Luggage stash—suitcases, duffel bags, carry-ons, old travel accessories hiding inside them.
Goal: Keep only usable, quality luggage and ditch the broken wheels, crusty zippers, and past-their-prime travel relics.

🗑 Letting Go Tip + Memory Keeper Tip

Letting Go Tip: If it's torn, cracked, missing wheels, or smells like it's been to the moon and back —it's time to retire it. That suitcase has served you well. Let it go with gratitude (and maybe Lysol).

Memory Keeper Tip: Find a meaningful travel item? A shell from your favorite beach or a postcard tucked in a zipper pocket? Pop it into your memory box. No one needs to store it inside an old gym bag for eternity.

🧺 Organising Advice

Open every bag—yes, even the gym duffel. Shake out crumbs, remove forgotten contents, and clean the linings. Stack smaller suitcases inside larger ones to save space (luggage nesting dolls = genius). Keep one solid carry-on, one medium, and one large if you actually use them. Donate or recycle the rest. Store accessories (travel bottles, neck pillows, adapters) in a labeled tote inside the suitcase you use most often.

Pro tip: If a bag hasn't been used since your last flip phone, it probably isn't your future.

💪 Mini Motivational Boost

Letting go of old luggage doesn't mean giving up on adventure. It just means you're ready to travel smarter —with less stuff, more freedom, and maybe a zipper that actually works. There's something powerful about knowing you could pack in five minutes and feel good about it.

Checklist for the Week

- Pull out all luggage, travel bags, and accessories
- Check for wear, damage, smells, broken wheels/zippers
- Toss or donate anything no longer functional or needed
- Clean out crumbs, sand, receipts, mystery tissues
- Nest smaller luggage into larger pieces
- Store travel accessories neatly inside your go-to suitcase
- Wipe down and organize storage area
- Daydream about your next trip (it counts as self-care)

One to Keep, One to Toss Challenge

Keep: Your most reliable, comfy-to-carry suitcase that still makes you feel travel-ready.
Toss: The duffel bag with the broken strap that smells like gym socks and despair.

Week 15: Bookshelf Backlog—Are You Really Going to Read That?

Books are sacred. They're comforting, inspiring, and smell weirdly amazing. But somewhere between "I love books" and "I need a forklift to dust this shelf," things got out of hand. I once found *three* copies of the same novel, none of which I'd actually read. Also: a diet book from 1996, a travel guide to Yugoslavia, and a self-help book I was clearly too lazy to finish.

We collect books with the best intentions—aspirational reading, gifts, spontaneous charity shop finds—but eventually, our shelves become a guilt shrine. This week, we sort the meaningful from the maybe-one-day. You don't have to read everything to be smart. Or keep everything to be sentimental.

🎯 The Weekly Declutter Focus

Target Zone: Bookshelves, bedside stacks, forgotten boxes, and "temporary" piles that became permanent.
Goal: Keep only the books you love, use, or genuinely intend to read. Free the rest to find new readers.

🗑 Letting Go Tip + Memory Keeper Tip

Letting Go Tip: Be honest. If you've moved the same unread book through three houses, it's not a future read—it's a paperweight. Keep books that make you feel something, not just shame.

Memory Keeper Tip: Got a book with a personal note, scribbled kid art inside, or sentimental value? Keep it in your memory stash or display it with pride. One well-loved book beats a pile of "maybe someday."

🧺 Organising Advice

Pull every book off the shelves. Yes, all of them. Group into categories: read/loved, want to read, donate, and "why do I still have this?" Wipe shelves down before restocking. Alphabetize, color-code, or stack by size—whatever makes your inner librarian happy. Donate good-condition books to local libraries, schools, or charity shops.

Create a small "to be read" shelf—and be realistic. No judgment, just honesty.

💪 Mini Motivational Boost

Books are meant to be read and shared—not hoarded out of guilt. By curating a meaningful collection, you're not giving up knowledge. You're giving it room to breathe. Plus, empty shelf space? That's power. That's potential. That's room for a plant.

Checklist for the Week

- Remove all books from shelves, drawers, and mystery piles
- Sort into: Keep, To Read, Donate, Sentimental
- Dust and wipe down all book surfaces and shelves
- Let go of duplicates, guilt-reads, and "meh" titles
- Donate or gift unused books to a good home
- Organize the ones you keep in a way that sparks joy (or at least isn't dusty)
- Create a small, doable "to be read" stack
- Celebrate with a hot drink and a good read

 One to Keep, One to Toss Challenge

Keep: The book you've read five times and would read five more.
Toss: The self-help guide you bought in a panic and never opened—your future doesn't need that pressure.

Week 16: The Over-the-Fridge Mystery Cabinet

Every home has one. That awkward, out-of-reach cabinet above the fridge that requires a step ladder, upper body strength, and the flexibility of a gymnast to access. Mine once contained a waffle maker, a bread machine manual (but no bread machine), and a single shot glass shaped like a flamingo. I hadn't opened it since my child was in braces.

This cabinet becomes the final resting place for items that don't belong anywhere else but feel "too useful to throw out." Spoiler: they're not. This week, we face it—possibly with goggles—and reclaim a bit of vertical sanity.

🎯 The Weekly Declutter Focus

Target Zone: That tall, usually-ignored cabinet above the refrigerator—or any hard-to-reach kitchen shelf that hides your culinary "somedays."
Goal: Clear out what you don't use, keep only what earns its place, and prevent future accidental Tupperware landslides.

🗑 Letting Go Tip + Memory Keeper Tip

Letting Go Tip: If you didn't know it was up there, you don't need it. Nostalgia is not a valid reason to store a fondue pot you forgot existed.

Memory Keeper Tip: Found something quirky with a fun family memory? Take a photo and write a note about the time you used it. Let the story live on—without the appliance.

🧺 Organising Advice

Use a sturdy chair or step stool to safely access the cabinet. Pull everything out (carefully—flying kitchen gadgets are real). Check for duplicates, broken tools, or items you haven't used in over a year. Only keep rarely used essentials (like a holiday platter or punch bowl). Store those in labeled bins or containers so nothing disappears into the cabinet void again.

Pro tip: If something doesn't fit easily or requires Tetris-level maneuvering—it doesn't belong there.

Mini Motivational Boost

Decluttering the high, hidden corners of your kitchen is a power move. It says, "I don't need to be burdened by forgotten gear or mystery gadgets." It's about bringing clarity and functionality—even to the places no one sees but you. And maybe avoiding a surprise avalanche next time you reach for the blender.

Decluttering for Empty Nesters

Checklist for the Week

- Grab a safe stool or ladder and open the cabinet
- Carefully remove all items (protect your head!)
- Sort into: Use Often, Rarely Use, Never Touch
- Toss or donate anything broken, redundant, or ridiculous
- Clean the inside of the cabinet (hello, mystery crumbs)
- Store rarely used items in bins or labeled containers
- Only return what fits easily and has a purpose
- Bask in the glory of an emptier, safer upper kitchen zone

One to Keep, One to Toss Challenge

Keep: The serving dish you only use once a year but genuinely love.
Toss: The waffle iron that doubles as a shoulder workout and hasn't made waffles since 2009.

Week 17: Bath Products That Retired Before You Did

There's nothing quite like a bathroom shelf full of "almost empty," "never opened," and "why is this sticky?" products. I once found a bottle of glitter body gel that was so ancient it had separated into layers—like a science experiment in regret. And let's not even discuss the bath bombs that now resemble dusty rocks from another planet.

We keep bath products with hope. Hope that we'll suddenly become people who exfoliate daily or finally take that long lavender-scented soak. But if your bathroom looks more like a skincare aisle hit by a tornado, it's time for a bubbly reset.

🎯 The Weekly Declutter Focus

Target Zone: Bathroom cabinets, shelves, shower caddies, window ledges—anywhere lotions, potions, and long-forgotten serums hide.
Goal: Keep only what you use and love. Toss the expired, separated, sticky, and mysterious.

🗑 Letting Go Tip + Memory Keeper Tip

Letting Go Tip: If it's expired, smells weird, separated into layers, or reminds you of a spa day that never happened—it's time to go. Your skin deserves better.

Memory Keeper Tip: If you find a scent that reminds you of a meaningful time, save just the cap or take a picture. You can remember the moment without storing a half-used bottle for eternity.

🧺 Organising Advice

Empty everything out of drawers, cabinets, and tubs. Group products into categories: daily use, occasional use, expired, and "what even is this?" Check expiry dates—yes, even soap can go funky. Wipe down shelves and lids (prepare for goo). Only put back what you actually use. Store backups together. Use small bins or baskets for categories like skincare, haircare, or bath time.

Pro tip: Limit products to what fits neatly in one drawer or shelf. If you need overflow bins for shampoo, we may need to talk.

💪 Mini Motivational Boost

Decluttering your bath products is about choosing care over clutter. It's saying yes to the things that nourish and no to the ones that guilt-trip you from the back of the shelf. Fewer options = less stress = more peaceful showers.

✅ Checklist for the Week

- Empty bathroom cabinets, drawers, and ledges
- Check all products for expiry, separation, or weird smells
- Toss anything unused in the last year or looking tragic
- Group items by use: daily, weekly, occasional
- Wipe down all surfaces and bottles
- Store essentials in reachable spots, backups in bins
- Keep it minimal: quality over quantity
- Reward yourself with an actual bath (maybe with a fresh bath bomb!)

🗑️ One to Keep, One to Toss Challenge

Keep: The luxurious lotion or body wash you *actually* love to use.

Toss: The crusty face mask from 2017 that now smells like regret and clay.

Week 18: Holiday Decorations That Should've Stayed in 1997

Somewhere in the back of a cupboard or loft lies a box you fear more than tax season: the Holiday Decorations Bin. You know the one. Inside, it's a tangled mess of lights that only half work, glittery reindeer missing legs, a melted candle shaped like a snowman (now just... a waxy snow blob), and approximately 92 feet of tangled tinsel from the Clinton era.

Decorations hold memories—we know that. But when your attic starts looking like Santa's storage unit after a nervous breakdown, it's time to sort the sparkle from the sprawl. This week, we let go of the cracked, faded, and "what even is this?" ornaments and keep only the magic.

🎯 The Weekly Declutter Focus

Target Zone: Holiday boxes, attic bins, under-the-stairs chaos caves—wherever festive stuff is stored. **Goal:** Curate a meaningful, manageable collection of decorations you actually use—and love.

🗑 Letting Go Tip + Memory Keeper Tip

Letting Go Tip: If it's broken, faded, tangled beyond repair, or hasn't made it out of the box since dial-up internet—you can let it go. It had its moment.

Memory Keeper Tip: Keep one or two deeply meaningful pieces: the ornament from baby's first Christmas, the decoration made in primary school. Store these safely and with intention—not just tossed in with a 1990s "Let It Snow" banner.

🧺 Organising Advice

Pull out every box and bin. Unwrap and inspect each item. Test all lights (brace yourself). Group decorations by holiday and condition. Toss broken or overly worn items. Donate good-condition extras you don't use. Use clear bins or labeled boxes for each holiday. Store by season to make decorating (and un-decorating) way less stressful next year.

And for the love of sanity—wrap lights around cardboard, not into a ball of doom.

💪 Mini Motivational Boost

Decluttering your holiday decorations makes room for joy, not just stuff. It helps you celebrate with intention—not obligation. Let go of the pressure to deck every hall and instead focus on the pieces that light you up (figuratively *and* literally).

✅ Checklist for the Week

- Pull out all holiday decor from every storage spot
- Unwrap and inspect every item for damage or wear
- Test lights and electronics (toss the half-lit strands)
- Sort by holiday or theme
- Keep only what you love and use
- Toss or donate decorations that are dated, damaged, or not your style
- Repack with care: clear bins, labels, wrapped cords
- Make a note of what (if anything) you *actually* need next year

🎁 One to Keep, One to Toss Challenge

Keep: That timeless ornament that makes you smile every year.
Toss: The glitter-covered pine cone you made during a 1997 craft meltdown and haven't hung since.

Week 19: The Craft Supply Explosion

Once upon a time, you were going to make things. Scrapbooks, birthday banners, maybe a knitted cactus or two. So you bought supplies—glue sticks, googly eyes, paint, paper, washi tape, felt in 17 shades of green. Then life got busy. Or messy. Or you realized you hate crafts. And now you have a bin (or seven) of chaos that could power a primary school art fair for a decade.

I once found a hot glue gun with fossilized glue in it, a set of glitter pens that leaked like sparkly tears, and 34 popsicle sticks. No plan. Just vibes. This week, we reclaim the drawer, the box, the bin—and the dignity.

🎯 The Weekly Declutter Focus

Target Zone: Craft bins, drawers, cupboards, or entire hobby room corners where paint and pipe cleaners have gone to retire.
Goal: Keep only usable, inspiring materials and say goodbye to dried-up, duplicated, and "what was I thinking?" items.

🗑 Letting Go Tip + Memory Keeper Tip

Letting Go Tip: If it's dried out, used once in 2011, or a supply for a project you never actually liked—it's clutter in disguise. Be honest about what sparks creativity vs. what sparks guilt.

Memory Keeper Tip: Save one finished project you're proud of or one set of supplies that genuinely makes you feel creative. Label and store it with love—not regret.

🧺 Organising Advice

Empty everything out. Group by type: paper, pens, glue, sewing, beads, fabric, tools. Test all pens, markers, and paints—dried-up equals out. Toss anything damaged, dirty, or unusable. Store remaining supplies in clear bins, labeled drawers, or a rolling cart. Keep only what fits in your chosen space—no overflow bins of broken dreams allowed.

Consider donating good-condition extras to schools, kids' clubs, or community centers—they'll be thrilled, and you'll be free.

💪 Mini Motivational Boost

Crafting should be fun, not guilt-inducing. You're allowed to change hobbies. You're allowed to keep just what makes you happy. You are not a failed Pinterest project—you're someone with the courage to create *space* again.

✅ Checklist for the Week

- Gather all craft supplies from every nook and bin
- Group by category (paints, paper, sewing, etc.)
- Test tools and supplies—toss anything dried, broken, or crusty
- Donate gently used extras to someone who'll use them
- Clean bins, drawers, and shelves
- Store keepers by category in labeled containers
- Choose a realistic amount of space for your supplies—and stick to it
- Treat yourself to a mini creative session with what's left

🎁 One to Keep, One to Toss Challenge

Keep: The supply or tool you actually *love* to use—hello, watercolor pencils.
Toss: That tangled ball of ribbon and guilt from your "gift-wrapping era."

Week 20: The Kids' Room Museum Exhibit

You know the room. The posters are still up. The trophies are still proudly displayed. The bookshelf hasn't been touched since Year 9, and there's a distinct scent of "old sneakers and teenage dreams." It's part bedroom, part shrine, part accidental time capsule.

I once opened a drawer in my kid's old room and found a dried-out lip balm, three broken earbuds, and a note that just said "Revenge Plan, Step 2." I never found Steps 1 or 3. But I did find an entire wardrobe full of clothes they outgrew a decade ago.

This week, we lovingly retire the past, refresh the space, and maybe make room for a proper guest bed —one that doesn't feature glow-in-the-dark bedsheets and a beanbag that wheezes when you sit down.

◎ The Weekly Declutter Focus

Target Zone: Your grown child's former bedroom—closets, drawers, under the bed, shelves, and maybe that one box they swore they'd come back for.
Goal: Preserve the meaningful, clear the clutter, and gently transition the space into something fresh (or at least functional).

Letting Go Tip + Memory Keeper Tip

Letting Go Tip: If it's broken, forgotten, stained, or so outgrown that it physically hurts to look at—it can go. You're not erasing their childhood. You're making room for the next chapter.

Memory Keeper Tip: Choose a few keepsakes: a favorite childhood book, a beloved toy, a piece of art or a note. Store them in a labeled memory box. Or better yet, ask your child to help pick what matters most.

Organising Advice

Start with one area at a time. Sort items into: keep for them, keep for you, donate, toss. Label boxes clearly. Keep one memory box (two max) per child. If your kid is available, invite them to help—or at least text them pictures and get a yes/no. Convert the room into a guest room, office, yoga space, or nap paradise. Whatever brings *you* peace now.

Pro tip: Be kind to yourself. This isn't just a room—it's a portal. But portals need vacuuming too.

💪 Mini Motivational Boost

You're not letting go of your child. You're just letting go of their high school hoodie collection and seven jars of dry nail polish. This is about honoring the past while claiming the present. You're allowed to make this space yours again—with love, not guilt.

Checklist for the Week

- Sort the closet: remove outgrown or unused clothes
- Go through drawers, under-bed storage, and shelves
- Separate items into: keep, donate, toss, memory box
- Invite your child (in-person or virtually) to weigh in on key items
- Clean and vacuum the room—maybe open a window of emotional release
- Decide the new purpose for the room
- Reorganize the space to reflect its new role
- Take a deep breath and appreciate your strength

🎁 One to Keep, One to Toss Challenge

Keep: The stuffed animal or keepsake that still makes you smile.
Toss: The dried-out pens, old receipts, and the mysterious sock fossil under the bed.

Week 21: Broken Electronics—Sentimental but Useless

You know the drawer. Or maybe it's a box. Or an entire shelf in the garage. It's where old phones, cracked tablets, long-dead remotes, and unidentified cables go to die. You tell yourself you'll "maybe fix it" or "wipe the data someday," but really—you're the curator of a private museum of obsolete electronics.

I once found a flip phone, a digital camera that needed AA batteries (four of them), and a Walkman. The Walkman still worked. I couldn't find a cassette, but I was impressed. That said, I don't need to store it forever just because it once played my heartbreak playlist from 1998.

This week, we pull the plug on broken gadgets and unnecessary tech nostalgia—and make space for functioning joy.

🎯 The Weekly Declutter Focus

Target Zone: Drawers, bins, shelves, or garage cabinets filled with outdated, broken, or "maybe useful" electronics and cords.
Goal: Keep only what works, what's current, or what genuinely gets used. Recycle or dispose of the rest.

🗑 Letting Go Tip + Memory Keeper Tip

Letting Go Tip: If you haven't turned it on in three years, can't find the charger, or it belongs to an operating system no longer supported by modern civilization—it goes.

Memory Keeper Tip: Snap a photo of the gadget that held memories (like your first phone or a camcorder from family holidays). Print the photo. Keep the memory, not the broken hardware.

🧺 Organising Advice

Gather all electronics into one space. Sort into piles: working, maybe-working, and "what even is this?" Test items if possible. Recycle old batteries and electronics at a proper facility (not the bin). Keep only what works and has a current use. Label cords and chargers that stay. Store everything in one small container or drawer. If it doesn't fit—it doesn't stay.

Pro tip: If you own more random remotes than you have TVs, it's time for a tech exorcism.

💪 Mini Motivational Boost

Letting go of dead tech doesn't erase the memories—it releases you from the weight of "maybe someday" projects. You are not your iPod Shuffle collection. You are a person with working Wi-Fi and a life to enjoy *right now*.

✅ Checklist for the Week

- Gather all old phones, cords, gadgets, remotes, chargers
- Test devices if possible
- Separate working vs. broken items
- Properly recycle broken electronics and old batteries
- Donate usable, functioning items to a local reuse center
- Label and store the few chargers and accessories you actually use
- Reduce down to one container or drawer of current tech
- Celebrate your freedom from electronic ghosts

🗑 One to Keep, One to Toss Challenge

Keep: The working charger or tool you use regularly and can't live without.
Toss: The broken phone you swore you'd wipe in 2014—farewell, old friend.

Decluttering for Empty Nesters

Week 22: Old Phones and Their 78 Chargers

Somewhere in your home lies a sacred stash of old phones. Cracked screens, mysterious passcodes, maybe a grainy selfie or two still trapped inside. And for every phone? A small army of tangled, mostly useless chargers. iPhone 3 charger, Blackberry cable, that chunky Nokia plug that could double as a weapon in a pinch—it's all still here, like a forgotten tech reunion.

I once found a charger I didn't even recognize. No label, no match, just a weird end that looked like it belonged to a spy gadget. I kept it for another two years. Just in case. (Spoiler: It matched *nothing*.)

This week, we let go of the guilt, the outdated tech, and the cords that never connect. Because your drawer deserves better. And so do your outlets.

🎯 The Weekly Declutter Focus

Target Zone: Phone drawers, charging stations, mystery cord boxes, junk drawers, and anywhere old phones and their charging friends are lurking.
Goal: Keep one backup phone (if needed) and only the chargers that fit your current tech. Ditch the rest.

🗑️ Letting Go Tip + Memory Keeper Tip

Letting Go Tip: If the phone doesn't turn on, is locked forever, or is missing a SIM card the size of a playing card—it's done. And if a cord hasn't matched anything in your home since 2010, it's just wire spaghetti.

Memory Keeper Tip: Before tossing an old phone, back up any photos or texts that make you smile. Then take a deep breath and let it go. The phone isn't the memory—it just held it for a while.

🧺 Organising Advice

Gather all old phones, cords, and charging gadgets into one space. Test what works. Identify what fits your current devices. Label those and store them in a tidy bag or drawer. Recycle dead phones and mismatched cords at an e-waste facility (many phone stores take them). Keep one emergency backup phone if you must—but label it, charge it, and don't store it with 17 mystery cables.

Pro tip: Zip-top bags and cord ties are your new best friends.

💪 Mini Motivational Boost

You are not obligated to carry the entire history of mobile technology in your junk drawer. Letting go of old phones and orphaned chargers is like deleting

3,000 digital tabs in your brain. More space, more clarity, more room for today.

Checklist for the Week

- Gather all old phones and charging cables
- Match chargers to working devices—label as needed
- Test phones and back up important photos or data
- Recycle or donate working but unused phones
- Properly dispose of non-working phones and cords
- Keep only necessary cords (and no duplicates)
- Store neatly in a labeled pouch or bin
- Enjoy the serenity of not untangling cables ever again

One to Keep, One to Toss Challenge

Keep: One labeled charger that you use regularly and know exactly what it belongs to.
Toss: The spaghetti monster of mystery cords you've been too afraid to deal with—cut the cord, literally.

Week 23: The Sock Orphanage— Where Do Their Mates Go?

Somewhere out there is a land where missing socks party together, laugh at our confusion, and live lint-free lives. Meanwhile, back home, we stare at drawers full of single socks, hoping their partners will magically reappear. They don't. They never do.

I once had an entire basket labeled "Socks in Waiting." It had 27 unmatched socks. Some of them hadn't had a partner since the Bush administration. And yet… I kept them. Just in case. This week, it's time to face the truth, let go of the lone survivors, and finally see the bottom of your sock drawer.

🎯 The Weekly Declutter Focus

Target Zone: Sock drawers, laundry baskets, under-bed monsters, and any rogue bags of single socks "waiting" for their long-lost loves.
Goal: Keep only socks that are in pairs, in good condition, and that you actually wear. Let the others go to sock heaven.

🗑 Letting Go Tip + Memory Keeper Tip

Letting Go Tip: If it's lost its match, has holes, is stretched out, or belongs to a child who now pays rent

—it's time. Let go with love and perhaps a ceremonial wave.

Memory Keeper Tip: Got a baby sock that melts your heart? Keep just one and label it. It doesn't need to live next to a crusty gym sock from 2003.

Organising Advice

Dump the whole drawer. Group socks by type: everyday, dressy, sport, fuzzy, novelty. Match up pairs and toss the damaged or unpaired ones. Consider investing in a few small baskets or drawer dividers to keep them sorted. Going forward, clip or wash socks in mesh laundry bags to prevent breakups in the wash.

Pro tip: White socks should be white. If they're greyish-pink and used to be sporty white, it's time to say goodbye.

Mini Motivational Boost

Matching socks may seem like a small win—but it's a *real* win. There's something deeply satisfying about grabbing two socks that actually match and aren't plotting to destroy your heels. Fewer socks = less sorting = happier mornings.

Checklist for the Week

- Empty all sock drawers, baskets, and bins
- Match every pair—toss or repurpose singles
- Discard socks with holes, saggy elastic, or mystery stains
- Sort remaining socks by type and frequency of use
- Store in dividers, boxes, or baskets
- Consider a sock-washing system to prevent future orphans
- Donate gently used, wearable socks if allowed locally
- Admire your drawer and feel 10% more put together

🎁 One to Keep, One to Toss Challenge

Keep: That comfy, go-to pair that hugs your feet and makes you feel cozy.
Toss: The lonely novelty sock with a faded flamingo and no hope of reunion.

Week 24: Fridge Magnet Mania

Remember when your fridge used to be a blank, peaceful appliance? Me neither. Somewhere along the way, it became a gallery of expired coupons, ancient takeout menus, dentist reminders from 2017, and magnets shaped like everything from flip-flops to flamingos.

I once found a magnet from a pizza place that closed ten years ago. Right next to it? A calendar from 2015, a child's drawing of what may have been a cat, and a magnet shaped like a lobster wearing sunglasses. I couldn't tell you why I kept it, but it had *been through things.*

This week, we peel off the past and give the fridge—and our brains—a cleaner, calmer view.

◎ The Weekly Declutter Focus

Target Zone: The refrigerator exterior and sides, plus any magnetic memo boards or cluttered metal surfaces in the kitchen.
Goal: Keep only current, useful, or joy-sparking magnets and paper items. The rest? It's time to un-stick.

🗑 Letting Go Tip + Memory Keeper Tip

Letting Go Tip: If the magnet's ugly, broken, advertising a business that no longer exists, or hasn't been looked at in six months—off it goes. Same with any paper it's holding that's no longer relevant.

Memory Keeper Tip: Found a sentimental magnet or old kid artwork? Snap a photo, or keep just one or two favorites in your memory box. You don't need the whole fridge door to remember a moment.

Organising Advice

Take everything off the fridge and sort into piles: magnets, paper, keepsakes, trash. Toss or recycle outdated papers. Keep only magnets that are functional or meaningful (limit: no more than one lobster in sunglasses). Consider a corkboard, magnetic memo board, or command center for essentials like schedules or reminders—and leave the fridge door for a cleaner look.

Wipe down the fridge door. Trust me, it's sticky.

Mini Motivational Boost

A decluttered fridge door clears more than just visual space—it quiets the background noise in your kitchen. Your fridge doesn't need to be the family command center. It can just be… a fridge. A beautiful, breathing, magnet-light masterpiece.

☑ Checklist for the Week

- Remove all magnets, notes, menus, and papers from fridge and sides
- Sort into: keep, toss, relocate, or digitize
- Recycle or shred outdated paper items
- Clean and wipe down the fridge doors and handles
- Return only the essentials or display-worthy magnets
- Consider a separate command board for reminders, menus, etc.
- Enjoy the peaceful stillness of your newly minimalist fridge front
- Treat yourself to a snack—you earned it

One to Keep, One to Toss Challenge

Keep: A magnet that makes you smile *every* time you see it (or holds up your child's masterpiece).
Toss: The faded takeout menu from a restaurant that changed its name three years ago.

Week 25: The Garage—Not Just for Regret and Cobwebs

The garage is the home's "everything else" drawer, only bigger and more emotionally confusing. Bikes with flat tires. Paint cans from the *before times*. Garden tools, broken fans, five coolers, and a box labeled "Camping Stuff" even though no one in the house has camped since 2004.

I once opened a bin and found… six tennis rackets. I've never played tennis. I can only assume they arrived through some sort of clutter osmosis. The garage is where projects go to nap and belongings go to witness protection. This week, we shake off the dust, face the piles, and reclaim the space—before the lawn chairs become nesting grounds for spiders with tenure.

🎯 The Weekly Declutter Focus

Target Zone: The garage—or any outdoor storage area filled with tools, gear, bins, "someday" projects, and what-ifs.
Goal: Create a usable, breathable, and safe space that stores only what serves your current life.

🗑 Letting Go Tip + Memory Keeper Tip

Letting Go Tip: If it's broken, rusted, hasn't been touched in years, or inspires more guilt than joy—it's time. You are not the designated storage site for all things heavy and dusty.

Memory Keeper Tip: Found a childhood bike or an old sports trophy that still makes you smile? Snap a photo or set it aside for your memory box. Don't let nostalgia clog your parking space.

🧺 Organising Advice

Start small—one zone at a time. Sort everything into categories: tools, gear, decor, paint, seasonal, sports, garden, toss, and donate. Sweep or vacuum as you go. Store like with like in clear bins, labeled shelves, or pegboards. Hang tools. Use hooks for bikes. Get rid of duplicates (nobody needs four rusty rakes). If it's dangerous or expired (old chemicals, ancient motor oil)—dispose of it properly.

And if you've been saving wood scraps "just in case," now is the time to ask: in case *what*?

💪 Mini Motivational Boost

The garage might seem overwhelming, but each box, bin, and broom you deal with is a declaration: "I'm not storing regret anymore." You're clearing space not just for your car—but for possibility. Who knows? You might even start parking in there again.

Checklist for the Week

- Clear a small section at a time—don't tackle it all at once
- Create piles: keep, donate, toss, recycle, hazardous waste
- Sweep and clean shelves, floor, and corners as you go
- Label bins and group items by category
- Hang frequently used tools or gear
- Recycle or dispose of old paint, chemicals, and broken equipment
- Celebrate when you can actually see the floor
- Bonus win: Fit a car, bike, or hobby zone in the cleared space

One to Keep, One to Toss Challenge

Keep: The one tool or piece of gear you actually use and know how to operate.
Toss: That sad folding chair with a tear and a raccoon-sized spider web.

Week 26: The Car Boot Full of Good Intentions

At some point, your car boot transformed. It stopped being a tidy, practical space for groceries and emergency jump leads… and became a rolling storage locker of "I'll drop that off soon," "Just in case," and "How long has that been back there?" I once found a reusable shopping bag filled with… more reusable shopping bags. It was like a bag-inception situation.

Also: one boot picnic blanket, two half-used bottles of screen wash, three crushed water bottles, and a charity shop donation bag that had been riding around with me longer than my spare tire. This week, we turn the boot from a clutter cave into an actual, functional space. Because a clear boot = a smoother ride (emotionally and mechanically).

🎯 The Weekly Declutter Focus

Target Zone: Car boot (a.k.a. trunk), back seats, side pockets—every hidden vehicle nook filled with forgotten belongings and well-meaning cargo.
Goal: Remove the old, organize the essentials, and keep only what you truly need for life on the go.

🗑 Letting Go Tip + Memory Keeper Tip

Letting Go Tip: If it's dirty, expired, broken, or hasn't served a purpose in months—it can go. Your car isn't a lost & found or mobile garage.

Memory Keeper Tip: Found a sweet drawing from your kid or a tiny forgotten souvenir from a road trip? Pop it into your home memory box—not the dusty cupholder.

🧺 Organising Advice

Take *everything* out of the boot. Yes, even that mystery blanket. Vacuum if needed. Group items into: car essentials (jumper cables, first aid, de-icer), shopping stuff (reusable bags), and donations or returns. Put non-essentials *in the house* or drop them off today (not someday). Use a car organizer or small bin to keep the essentials from rolling around. Bonus: stash a trash bag in the boot for future car clutter emergencies.

Pro tip: If you could survive a week-long road trip based on your boot contents alone… it might be too much.

Mini Motivational Boost

Your car is not a mobile closet. Or a rolling recycling bin. By clearing your boot, you create space for actual freedom—spontaneous trips, clean slates, and a lot less rattling when you go around corners.

✅ Checklist for the Week

- Empty the entire boot and any storage compartments
- Toss trash, expired items, and random junk
- Return rogue items to the house where they belong
- Drop off long-delayed donation bags or returns
- Wipe down surfaces and vacuum if needed
- Group car essentials into a small organizer/bin
- Add a small emergency kit and reusable bags
- Close the boot with smug satisfaction and go for a little drive

🎁 One to Keep, One to Toss Challenge

Keep: A compact, practical emergency kit or reusable bag that actually gets used.
Toss: That random box of "stuff" you've been meaning to sort for the last two Christmases.

Week 27: The Mystery Cupboard You Haven't Opened Since 2011

Every house has one. That strange, shadowy cupboard you've walked past for years but haven't opened because... well, you forgot what's even in there. Maybe it's near the stairs. Maybe it's high up. Maybe it's that awkward corner cabinet that requires full-body origami to access. Wherever it is, it has the aura of *forgotten things and mild concern*.

I opened ours once and found: one VHS tape (we have no player), three mismatched lamp shades, a fondue fork, and a box labeled "Stuff." No further details. Also: a petrified jellybean. Possibly vintage.

This week, we face the cupboard with courage, curiosity, and possibly a dust mask. Because what's the point of keeping space you never use?

🎯 The Weekly Declutter Focus

Target Zone: That one cupboard, shelf, or corner storage area you've avoided, forgotten, or sworn to deal with "later" since at least 2011.
Goal: Open it, sort it, clear it. Turn mystery storage into meaningful space.

🗑 Letting Go Tip + Memory Keeper Tip

Letting Go Tip: If you forgot you owned it, haven't needed it in a decade, or immediately felt regret upon touching it—it's probably not essential.

Memory Keeper Tip: Found something unexpectedly sentimental (like a childhood toy or a tucked-away letter)? Keep it with intention—in a memory box, not buried behind a broken lamp.

Organising Advice

Take *everything* out (brace for dust and a few "What the...?" moments). Sort into: keep, donate, toss, and memory. Be honest about what serves you today—not ten years ago. Clean the space well, especially if it hasn't seen light since broadband was dial-up. Then decide what the space *could* be used for: seasonal decor? Extra linens? A secret snack stash?

Pro tip: If you hesitate and think, "This might be useful someday," ask yourself, "Has it been useful *any* day since 2011?"

Mini Motivational Boost

Tackling forgotten storage is like unearthing buried treasure—or releasing buried guilt. You're not just clearing a cupboard, you're claiming hidden square footage and turning "meh" space into magic.

✅ Checklist for the Week

- Open the mystery cupboard with bravery (and maybe gloves)
- Remove all items and sort into categories
- Toss anything broken, irrelevant, or long-forgotten
- Rehome sentimental items in your memory box
- Clean the inside (hello, cobwebs and dust bunnies)
- Decide what, if anything, should be stored there now
- Return only useful, needed items neatly
- Reward yourself with tea, a biscuit, and zero regret

🎁 One to Keep, One to Toss Challenge

Keep: A forgotten treasure that still brings you genuine joy.
Toss: That tangled bundle of outdated tech cords, mystery bolts, or broken mini blinds.

Week 28: The Linen Closet—Towels That Have Seen Too Much

There's something oddly intimate about the linen closet. It starts out fresh and hopeful—perfect stacks of fluffy towels, neatly folded sheets, the occasional lavender sachet. Fast forward a few years, and it's a squashed chaos zone of mystery pillowcases, fitted sheets that bite, and towels that feel like sandpaper.

I once pulled out a towel I thought was beige. It was originally white. It had been through... things. Found beneath it? A queen-sized fitted sheet, even though we haven't owned a queen bed since the Spice Girls were topping charts.

This week, we give the linens some love. We let go of what's worn and forgotten, and make space for softness, simplicity, and shelves that don't collapse every time you grab a flannel.

🎯 The Weekly Declutter Focus

Target Zone: Linen closets, hallway cupboards, or wherever you store towels, sheets, blankets, pillowcases, and other fabric-based household frienemies.
Goal: Keep only what you use, need, and enjoy. Donate the rest—or upgrade the dog's towel collection.

Letting Go Tip + Memory Keeper Tip

Letting Go Tip: If it's stained, scratchy, smells faintly like your college dorm, or hasn't been used since "Downton Abbey" Season 1—it's time. Your skin (and house guests) deserve better.
Memory Keeper Tip: Sentimental baby blanket? Grandmother's handmade quilt? Absolutely keep it—but store it with care in a labeled memory box or special shelf. Not shoved behind the guest towels.

Organising Advice

Pull everything out. Yes, all of it. Group by type: bath towels, hand towels, face cloths, sheet sets, pillowcases, seasonal blankets. Check for damage, mismatches, and "what bed does this even fit?" moments. Fold and stack neatly by category. Use shelf bins or labeled baskets for small items like pillowcases or flannels. Store sheet sets inside their matching pillowcase for genius-level neatness.

Pro tip: Two sheet sets per bed and two towels per person is usually plenty—with a few extras for guests or emergencies.

💪 Mini Motivational Boost

Your linen closet should make you feel calm, not confused. Letting go of overstuffed, mismatched, mystery fabrics creates space for rest and simplicity. And yes—your towels can spark joy. Or at least stop scratching you.

✅ Checklist for the Week

- Empty out your entire linen closet or linen storage
- Sort by type and size: towels, sheets, pillowcases, blankets
- Check for damage, musty smells, stains, and wear
- Donate or repurpose old linens (animal shelters love them!)
- Fold and stack by category or use bins/baskets for sorting
- Store sheet sets inside pillowcases for easy grabbing
- Label shelves if needed—especially in shared homes
- Step back and admire your hotel-worthy linen stash

🎁 One to Keep, One to Toss Challenge

Keep: The towel that still feels like a warm hug and actually dries things.
Toss: The crispy old beach towel that smells like chlorine and regret.

Week 29: The Filing Cabinet Full of Paper That's Not Even Yours

Paper has a sneaky way of multiplying. One minute you're filing a few important documents, and the next thing you know, your filing cabinet is groaning under the weight of old warranties, expired insurance policies, birthday cards from people you can't identify, and your child's Year 6 maths homework—despite the fact they're now married with a mortgage.

I once found a manual for a DVD player we no longer owned, a receipt for a toaster from 2008, and a single printed email that just said "LOL." Why? No idea. And half the paperwork wasn't even mine. This week, we sort, shred, and streamline.

🎯 The Weekly Declutter Focus

Target Zone: Filing cabinets, paperwork drawers, folders, envelopes stuffed in weird places, and the "safe place" where documents go to disappear.
Goal: Keep only the essential, current, and legally necessary paperwork. Recycle or shred the rest.

🗑 Letting Go Tip + Memory Keeper Tip

Letting Go Tip: If it's expired, duplicated, irrelevant, or belongs to a vacuum cleaner you tossed five years ago—let it go. You are not the archivist of appliance history.

Memory Keeper Tip: For sentimental paper (like handwritten letters or precious cards), keep only your favorites in a labeled keepsake folder—not mixed in with tax returns and dog vaccination records.

🧺 Organising Advice

Sort everything into piles: To Keep, To Shred, To Recycle, and To Question ("Why do I have a fax from 2003?"). Only keep documents that are:
- Legally required (e.g. taxes, medical, wills)
- Actively useful (e.g. warranties, insurance)
- Meaningful (e.g. letters, certificates)

Label folders clearly: **Home**, **Health**, **Finance**, **Pets**, etc. Consider scanning important docs and storing them digitally (and safely). Shred anything with personal details before recycling.

Pro tip: You probably don't need to keep every utility bill you've paid since 2006. Just saying.

Mini Motivational Boost

Paper clutter is sneaky, overwhelming, and oddly heavy. By tackling it head-on, you're not just clearing space—you're creating peace of mind. No more digging for that one form when you need it. You've got this... in alphabetical order.

Checklist for the Week

- Empty out all paper piles, folders, drawers, and dusty envelopes
- Sort into: Keep, Shred, Recycle, Memory
- Toss expired or irrelevant documents (responsibly)
- Shred anything with personal info
- Label and file what remains clearly and simply
- Create a small memory folder for meaningful paper keepsakes
- Clean drawers or filing cabinets before returning items
- Breathe deeply—you've conquered the paper beast

🗑 One to Keep, One to Toss Challenge

Keep: The one document you always struggle to find—put it in a labeled folder today.
Toss: The expired travel brochure from 2011 still promising "exotic adventures" and paper cuts.

Week 30: The Recipe Collection That Hasn't Seen an Oven Since 1999

Once upon a time, you were going to make sourdough from scratch, learn 25 ways to roast a chicken, and host a dinner party that would make Nigella weep with joy. So you clipped recipes, printed Pinterest masterpieces, and kept cookbooks like sacred tomes. Fast forward a few years, and your "recipe collection" is a half-burnt binder, a drawer full of grease-stained papers, and cookbooks you've never opened beyond the index.

I once found a handwritten recipe card titled "Linda's Thing" with no instructions, just "bake until it smells done." I don't know who Linda is. I've never baked her thing. But I saved that card for six years. Why? No one knows.

This week, we declutter the dishes we'll never cook, organize the meals we love, and create a recipe system that works for how you actually eat—not how you planned to eat during that brief paleo phase.

◎ The Weekly Declutter Focus

Target Zone: Recipe binders, cookbooks, folders, printed recipe piles, clipped magazine pages, digital screenshots, and scribbled notes on the backs of envelopes.

Goal: Keep a curated collection of recipes you *actually use*. Let go of the culinary clutter.

Letting Go Tip + Memory Keeper Tip

Letting Go Tip: If you've never made it, wouldn't make it now, or it calls for ingredients you'd have to import from another planet—it's time to let it go. Aspirational cooking is fine. Guilt-cooking is not.

Memory Keeper Tip: Got a family recipe card in Grandma's handwriting? Keep that one forever. Maybe even frame it. Let legacy live—but don't let it get lost under a stack of "clean keto sheet pan dinners."

Organising Advice

Gather all recipes—physical and digital. Sort into categories: **Keep & Use**, **Maybe Someday**, **Why Did I Save This?**, and **Legacy Treasures**. Be ruthless with random clippings and old printouts. Create a binder, folder, or digital file system for the recipes that stay. Label categories clearly (e.g. Quick Dinners, Baking, Holiday, Go-To Favourites). Consider using plastic sleeves for handwritten or messy recipes you love.

Pro tip: No one needs four separate banana bread recipes. Pick your winner and donate the rest to the compost bin.

Mini Motivational Boost

This isn't just about tossing paper—it's about reclaiming your kitchen inspiration. When your recipe collection reflects your real taste, lifestyle, and energy levels, cooking becomes a joy again—not a guilt trip with 37 loose-leaf lasagna instructions.

Checklist for the Week

- Gather every recipe from every dusty drawer, cookbook pile, and browser tab
- Sort into: Keep, Toss, Memory, and Maybe
- Recycle old clippings, printouts, or duplicate dishes
- Digitize your favourites or store in a clean, simple binder
- Protect family heirloom recipes in sleeves or memory boxes
- Label clearly by type of meal or frequency of use
- Store within easy reach for actual cooking
- Celebrate by making something you actually *want* to cook

One to Keep, One to Toss Challenge

Keep: The go-to meal you've made a hundred times and still love (hello, lasagna of legends).
Toss: The five-page mushroom soufflé that requires a

blowtorch, two sous-chefs, and a life you do not currently live.

Week 31: The Gift Wrap Explosion

It starts with a roll of holiday wrap and some tape. Then comes the tissue paper, the gift bags (so many gift bags), the slightly smushed bows, the tags that don't stick, and ribbon that now looks more like yarn's regretful cousin. Before you know it, you've got a whole shelf, bin, or closet full of half-used wrapping paper, mysterious crinkly bits, and glitter that will never leave your home.

I once found gift wrap that said "Happy 2009" on it. Also: a wedding card with no envelope, and a tangled knot of curling ribbon that looked like it had been in a fight. It lost.

This week, we sort, recycle, and organize the festive fluff. Because celebrating others shouldn't come with its own storage crisis.

🎯 The Weekly Declutter Focus

Target Zone: Gift wrap supplies—paper rolls, bags, ribbons, bows, tags, boxes, cards, and anything else that's ever been slapped onto a present.
Goal: Keep only what's in good shape, current, and actually gets used. Organize it so you can find it *before* the next birthday panic.

🗑️ Letting Go Tip + Memory Keeper Tip

Letting Go Tip: If it's torn, faded, bent, or covered in last year's tape—it's time. Also, if you've been saving a tiny sliver of paper for "just the right gift," but haven't found it in five years… it's probably not coming.

Memory Keeper Tip: If you've got a tag or card that meant something—like a heartfelt note or a drawing by a kid—pop it into your keepsake box. Don't let it get bent under old Santa wrap.

🧺 Organising Advice

Empty your entire gift wrap zone and sort by category: paper rolls, bags, ribbons, tags, cards, boxes. Recycle or bin anything damaged or sad. Use a hanging organizer, a tall bin for wrap rolls, and small containers for bows, ribbon, and tags. Store by occasion (birthday, holiday, etc.) and label if you want bonus points. Keep one small container of neutral wrap for emergencies—you're not running a gift shop.

Pro tip: You do not need to save every single bag you receive. You're not preparing for a retail flashback.

💪 Mini Motivational Boost

Giving gifts should feel joyful—not like you're digging through the ruins of Wrapping Past. By simplifying your gift wrap stash, you'll make it easier to celebrate—and stress less when you're out of tape (again).

Checklist for the Week

- Gather all wrapping paper, bags, ribbon, tags, tape, and cards
- Sort into: keep, toss, recycle, repurpose
- Discard anything torn, crumpled, outdated, or unused in years
- Organize by occasion and type (paper, bags, ribbon, tags)
- Use bins, baskets, or hanging organizers for storage
- Store neutrals together for grab-and-go gift wrap emergencies
- Wipe down storage area and clear space for easy access
- Do a celebratory wrap of literally anything—just because you can

One to Keep, One to Toss Challenge

Keep: A few rolls of paper and bags you actually use and love (bonus if they match).
Toss: The wrinkled paper scraps and squashed bows from three birthdays ago.

Week 32: The Medicine Cabinet Mystery Tour

The medicine cabinet always *starts* with good intentions. A box of plasters. Some paracetamol. Maybe a neatly labeled bottle of vitamins. But over time, it becomes a cluttered medley of half-used ointments, expired allergy pills, a cough syrup bottle that's permanently sticky, and one mystery cream with a label so faded you're afraid to touch it.

I once found five packets of cold medicine, all expired. All different brands. All missing the dosing leaflet. Oh, and a thermometer that hasn't worked since the early 2000s. It was a health hazard disguised as health care.

This week, we clear the cabinet, check the dates, and make space for what actually works—without fear of accidentally ingesting 12-year-old antacids.

🎯 The Weekly Declutter Focus

Target Zone: Medicine cabinets, bathroom drawers, kitchen cupboards, or wherever you store medications, supplements, and first-aid supplies.
Goal: Keep only current, safe, and necessary medical supplies. Safely dispose of the rest.

🗑 Letting Go Tip + Memory Keeper Tip

Letting Go Tip: If it's expired, unlabelled, sticky, broken, or no longer prescribed to anyone in the household—out it goes. Medication is not sentimental. It's not wine—it doesn't get better with age.

Memory Keeper Tip: None this week! Medications are not memory items. But if you find a hospital wristband or birth tag with emotional value, move that to your memory box—not next to the Vicks Vaporub.

🧺 Organising Advice

Pull out *everything*. Check expiry dates. Toss anything past its prime, open too long, or unidentifiable. Separate into categories: daily meds, cold/flu, pain relief, first aid, allergies, travel, etc. Use labeled containers, small baskets, or zip pouches for each category. Store away from heat and humidity (so maybe not the steamy bathroom after all).

Take expired medicine to your local pharmacy for safe disposal—don't toss it in the bin or flush it.

Mini Motivational Boost

Having a clean, organized medicine cabinet gives you more than space—it gives you peace of mind. The next time someone says "Do we have any plasters?" you'll know the answer without a twenty-minute archaeological dig through sticky boxes.

Checklist for the Week

- Remove everything from your medicine cabinet or storage area
- Check expiry dates and toss anything out of date or unidentifiable
- Safely dispose of expired meds at a pharmacy
- Wipe down shelves and sticky bottles
- Group items into logical categories (pain, cold/flu, first aid, etc.)
- Store in labeled bins, pouches, or containers
- Keep daily-use meds easily accessible
- Restock any essential items you're out of (like plasters or paracetamol)

 ## One to Keep, One to Toss Challenge

Keep: The up-to-date, go-to medication you reach for when life happens.
Toss: The cough syrup with a crusty cap that expired during the Olympics. (Two Olympics ago.)

Week 33: The Jewellery Box Time Forgot

Your jewellery box holds stories—first dates, weddings, kids' handmade bead creations, and that one necklace you bought on holiday and *swore* you'd wear all the time (you didn't). But now? It's a tangled time capsule of single earrings, broken clasps, and mystery chains that may or may not be gold. Also: plastic rings from 1998, several mystery keys, and a mood ring that's permanently stuck on "mildly stressed."

I once found a bracelet in mine that I was convinced I'd lost years ago. Turns out it was just hiding beneath seventeen pairs of green faux-pearl earrings (why? no idea). This week, we shine a light into the box and reclaim the sparkle.

🎯 The Weekly Declutter Focus

Target Zone: Jewellery boxes, trays, travel pouches, mystery drawers, and anywhere shiny things go to get tangled and forgotten.
Goal: Keep only what you wear, love, or cherish. Let go of the rest—or repurpose it with joy.

🗑 Letting Go Tip + Memory Keeper Tip

Letting Go Tip: If it's broken and you won't fix it, a mystery metal you're allergic to, or hasn't seen the light of day since the early 2000s—it's time to let it go. Guilt isn't a good accessory.

Memory Keeper Tip: Keep a few sentimental pieces—even if you don't wear them—like a locket from a loved one or your child's first macaroni necklace. Store them separately in a labeled keepsake pouch so they don't tangle with your day-to-day sparkle.

🧺 Organising Advice

Lay out everything. Untangle the mess (yes, patience and tea required). Sort into categories: daily wear, occasion, sentimental, donate, repair, toss. Polish the pieces that deserve to shine again. Consider a drawer insert, hanging organiser, or stackable trays to separate and store by use or style. Use little bags or boxes to keep chains from re-tangling.

Pro tip: Keep a small dish or tray near where you take jewellery off most often—your bathroom sink does *not* count.

💪 Mini Motivational Boost

Decluttering your jewellery isn't about being fancy—it's about honouring what you actually love and use. Every time you reach for a piece that fits your style and feels good, you're reminding yourself that *you* are the treasure worth adorning.

Checklist for the Week

- Gather all jewellery from drawers, boxes, bags, and trays
- Untangle necklaces and group like items together
- Sort into: keep, sentimental, donate, repair, toss
- Wipe, polish, or clean anything worth keeping
- Use organisers or dividers to keep items separate and visible
- Set aside broken items for repair—or finally admit they're done
- Store sentimental pieces away from daily-use chaos
- Celebrate your decluttered sparkle with your favourite piece today

🎁 One to Keep, One to Toss Challenge

Keep: The piece that makes you feel fabulous every time you wear it.
Toss: The lone earring that's been "waiting for its mate" for seven years and counting.

Week 34: That Drawer Full of Chargers, Cables, and Confusion (Yes, Another One)

We've all got one. That tech drawer (or bin, or bag, or box) that was *meant* to keep you organized… and now looks like it belongs in a crime scene investigation titled *"Cords Gone Wild."* Inside: charger ends no one recognizes, outdated phone plugs, mystery USBs, defunct power banks, and approximately 17 earbuds that may or may not work.

I once pulled out a cable that looked like it belonged to a camcorder. We've never owned a camcorder. Also found: a car phone charger for a car I sold in 2015. Somewhere in that chaos? The one charger I was actually looking for—tangled around a mouse (the tech kind, not the rodent).

This week, we tackle the wire nest and sort out your charging life once and for all.

🎯 The Weekly Declutter Focus

Target Zone: Tech drawers, bins, cable baskets, "gadget graveyard" boxes—anywhere chargers and cables go to get tangled and multiply.
Goal: Keep only cords and gadgets you actually use. Label them. Store them smart. And ditch the wire spaghetti.

Letting Go Tip + Memory Keeper Tip

Letting Go Tip: If you don't know what it connects to, haven't used it in years, or it belongs to tech that no longer lives here—it's time to part ways. Chargers don't have sentimental value. They have dust.

Memory Keeper Tip: None needed this week (unless you find a love letter typed into a 2004 Palm Pilot—but even then, digitize it). This is about clearing clutter, not saving nostalgia.

Organising Advice

Dump all cords and gadgets onto a table. Match chargers to devices (test if needed). Group by type: phone chargers, laptop cords, USB cables, headphones, HDMI, etc. Use cable ties, rubber bands, or Velcro to tidy up. Label each one using washi tape or tiny tags. Use small boxes or drawer organizers to keep them separated. And designate *one* spot in your home for cords going forward.

Pro tip: Keep only one spare of each type—unless you run a charging café.

💪 Mini Motivational Boost

Taming your tech clutter makes life smoother every day. No more cable chaos. No more mystery adapters. Just clearly labeled, neatly coiled calm. Honestly, it's kind of… electrifying.

Checklist for the Week

- Empty the entire tech drawer, bin, or box
- Untangle and sort all cords by type
- Match cables to devices—test if needed
- Recycle or safely dispose of dead, frayed, or mystery cords
- Label each keeper cord or cable clearly
- Use ties, clips, or bands to prevent future tangles
- Store neatly in a box, drawer, or organizer
- Create a single "tech zone" for future sanity

🗑 One to Keep, One to Toss Challenge

Keep: The cable that charges your current phone quickly and reliably.
Toss: The ancient, unidentified plug you've been moving house to house like it's a family heirloom.

Week 35: The Pet Stuff Overflow Zone

Pets bring us joy, snuggles, and... an avalanche of gear. Collars, leads, beds, coats, squeaky toys, non-squeaky toys (that used to be squeaky), grooming tools, and at least one outfit you swore was "just for the Christmas photo." Over time, the pet corner becomes the pet *sprawl*. I once found three half-eaten rawhide bones and a squeaky donut wedged behind the washing machine. I don't even remember buying the donut.

This week, we honor your furry (or feathery, or scaly) friend by decluttering the pet supply pile into something that works for both of you—and smells significantly less like mystery kibble.

🎯 The Weekly Declutter Focus

Target Zone: Pet supplies drawer, cupboard, corner, bin—or wherever your animal's accessories, toys, and forgotten treats gather.
Goal: Keep only what your pet actually uses or needs. Toss the chewed, crusty, expired, or unnecessary.

Letting Go Tip + Memory Keeper Tip

Letting Go Tip: If it's torn, unsafe, never used, or expired—it's time to go. Guilt doesn't belong in the toy bin. Neither does that crunchy old treat packet from 2020.

Memory Keeper Tip: Got a favorite puppy toy or a collar from your first pet? Absolutely save it—but place it in your memory box, not the slobbery toy pile.

🧺 Organising Advice

Gather *everything*. Sort into categories: toys, grooming, feeding, clothes (if applicable), walking gear, medical, treats. Toss anything broken, expired, or ignored. Wash and sanitize toys and dishes. Use baskets, hooks, and bins to keep supplies accessible but tidy. Store only the essentials where you need them—like leads near the door and food near the bowls.

Pro tip: A rotating toy system (a few out at a time) keeps your pet excited and your floor less cluttered.

💪 Mini Motivational Boost

Decluttering your pet's stuff isn't just about tidiness—it's about making daily life smoother for both of you. A clear system = fewer last-minute searches for leads and no more digging through a fur-filled drawer for meds. Plus, your pet gets to rediscover the toys that were buried beneath the "meh" ones.

Checklist for the Week

- Gather all pet toys, accessories, food, meds, and gear
- Toss anything broken, worn out, or expired
- Sort into: toys, grooming, feeding, walking, clothes, health
- Clean bowls, leashes, toys, and storage bins
- Rehome unused supplies (shelters love donations!)
- Store essentials by zone: walk station, feeding area, etc.
- Create a dedicated bin or basket for toys in rotation
- Give your pet a freshly washed favorite toy as a bonus treat

One to Keep, One to Toss Challenge

Keep: That one toy your pet always grabs first.
Toss: The sad, stuffing-less bear that's more bacteria than bear.

Anissa Brodon

Week 36: That Drawer of Paper Bags, Plastic Bags, and Totes

We all do it. We save "just a few" plastic bags because they're useful. Then we add a few paper ones. And reusable totes. Then one from that fancy store, and another because "it folds so small!" Suddenly, you open the drawer and an avalanche of bags flutters out like a grocery-themed confetti cannon.

I once counted mine. I had 48 plastic bags, 19 paper ones (some with suspicious grease stains), and 14 tote bags—7 of which I never used because they were too small, too stiff, or smelled like regret. This week, we declutter your bag stash so that you're prepared… but not buried.

🎯 The Weekly Declutter Focus

Target Zone: That one drawer, cabinet, or cupboard where you store plastic bags, paper sacks, gift bags, and reusable totes.
Goal: Keep a functional, realistic collection. Ditch the squashed, ripped, or rarely-used extras.

🗑 Letting Go Tip + Memory Keeper Tip

Letting Go Tip: If it's torn, sticky, has a hole, smells weird, or hasn't been used in over a year—it can go.

Decluttering for Empty Nesters

You only need enough to handle a week's worth of errands, not an environmental emergency.

Memory Keeper Tip: If a bag reminds you of a fun trip or a meaningful moment (like a special shop or city souvenir), repurpose it as a keepsake folder or frame the logo as quirky art. Don't let it get lost in the bag landslide.

🧺 Organising Advice

Dump the entire collection onto the floor or table. Group by type: plastic, paper, reusable. Pick a number limit: e.g., 10 plastic, 5 paper, 3 totes that actually work. Recycle or donate the rest. Store plastic bags inside one bag (like a dispenser), paper bags stacked, and reusable totes folded and clipped together. Keep them in an easy-to-grab spot near the door or in the car.

Pro tip: If you need a backup for "just in case," it shouldn't take up half a cupboard.

💪 Mini Motivational Boost

This is more than a bag purge—it's a tiny act of control in a world of constant grocery runs. Fewer bags means more space, more sanity, and zero stress when you're heading out the door. No more plastic puffball wars. Just easy, grab-and-go living.

✅ Checklist for the Week

- Gather all plastic, paper, and reusable bags
- Check each for rips, dirt, weird smells, or wear
- Recycle or repurpose damaged or excessive bags
- Choose a realistic number of each type to keep
- Nest plastic bags into one for compact storage
- Stack paper bags neatly by size
- Fold and clip totes together or hang near your exit
- Place a few totes in your car or handbag for shopping trips

🗑 One to Keep, One to Toss Challenge

Keep: Your favorite, roomy tote that never lets you down.
Toss: The wrinkly, ripped plastic bag that looks like it's lived a full life… twice.

Week 37: The Perfume, Cologne, and Body Spray Graveyard

Once upon a time, you had a favorite fragrance. Then came the gifts, the samples, the impulse buys, the "it was on sale" bottles, and the *mysterious mists* you're 95% sure were meant for teenagers. Fast forward, and you've now got a perfume shelf that smells like a department store exploded during prom season.

I once found a bottle so old the liquid inside had turned yellow and separated. The label was missing, but it smelled like teenage heartbreak and melon. Deeply unsettling. This week, we reclaim the space and keep only the scents that still suit who you are *now*—not who you were when body glitter was a personality.

🎯 The Weekly Declutter Focus

Target Zone: Vanity tops, drawers, shelves, bathroom cabinets—wherever perfume, cologne, and body sprays go to fade and multiply.
Goal: Keep the fragrances you love and actually wear. Let go of expired, overpowering, or "who even gave me this?" bottles.

🗑️ Letting Go Tip + Memory Keeper Tip

Letting Go Tip: If it's expired, smells different than it used to, gives you a headache, or is just *not your vibe anymore*—let it go. Scent is personal. Not every bottle deserves to stick around forever.

Memory Keeper Tip: If a fragrance holds a strong emotional memory, but you no longer wear it, keep the bottle (or just the label) in your memory box, not your daily lineup.

🧺 Organising Advice

Gather all your fragrance bottles and spritzers in one place. Sniff-test each one (lightly!) and notice your immediate reaction: love it, meh, or *ew, why?* Group keepers by use—daily, special occasion, seasonal. Store them in a cool, dry place away from direct sunlight (which breaks down fragrance over time). If you want to display them, keep the collection curated—not cluttered.

Pro tip: Less really is more when it comes to scent. One signature fragrance beats twelve almost-empties.

Mini Motivational Boost

Scent is powerful—it evokes moods, memories, and moments. Keeping only the fragrances that make you feel fabulous is like wearing invisible confidence. Let go of old bottles and make space for who you *are*, not who you *used to be* (or who your aunt thought you were in 2008).

Checklist for the Week

- Gather all perfumes, colognes, and sprays from every corner
- Test each one for freshness and your current taste
- Toss or recycle anything that smells off, causes irritation, or feels outdated
- Clean bottle tops and wipe down your display area
- Organize by frequency of use or season
- Store away from heat and direct sunlight
- Consider decanting favorite scents into a travel-size atomizer
- Enjoy smelling like your best self, not a confused air freshener

One to Keep, One to Toss Challenge

Keep: The fragrance that makes you feel powerful, pretty, or peaceful.
Toss: The gift set spray that smells like a nightclub and regret.

Week 38: The Candle and Wax Melt Takeover

Candles start with innocent intentions. "This will make the house feel cozy," you say. Then suddenly you've got a drawer full of cinnamon apple, tropical breeze, mystery vanilla, "Autumn Leaves" (which smells nothing like leaves), and at least one candle that smells like regret and bath bombs. Oh, and the wax melts. So many cubes. So many scents. So many unidentifiable blobs of wax fused to the bottom of drawers.

I once found a candle labeled "Frosted Cupcake Delight." It was neither frosted, nor delightful. Also found: six tealights, all half-burned, none in holders. And a wax melt shaped like a snowflake… in July.

This week, we melt away the mess, keep what you *actually burn*, and make space for fragrances that truly bring comfort—not confusion.

🎯 The Weekly Declutter Focus

Target Zone: Candle collections, wax melt drawers, cupboards of seasonal scents, old candle holders, and mystery tealights.
Goal: Keep the scents you genuinely enjoy and use. Let go of dusty, unused, or overpowering stockpiles of waxy intentions.

Letting Go Tip + Memory Keeper Tip

Letting Go Tip: If it's been sitting for years, half-burned, has no scent left, or smells like synthetic despair—it's time to let it go. You are not a candle historian.

Memory Keeper Tip: If one scent reminds you of a meaningful moment, write that down or take a photo of the candle before tossing the stub. Memories are wonderful. Melted wax is not.

Organising Advice

Gather all candles, wax melts, holders, lighters, and accessories into one place. Sort by scent category: floral, fruity, spicy, seasonal, etc. Check burnability—if it's burned unevenly, has no wick left, or crumbles like pastry, it's done. Wipe down holders, recycle empty jars, and keep candles you'll actually burn. Store in a cool, dry place. Consider displaying just a few favorites and rotating seasonally.

Pro tip: You do not need a "spring scent" collection that requires its own shelf. Two or three great ones will do just fine.

💪 Mini Motivational Boost

Candles are for joy, peace, and lovely-smelling moments—not guilt and dust. Decluttering your candle stash clears mental space and makes room for slow evenings and warm glows—not just cluttered corners that smell like six competing body sprays.

✅ Checklist for the Week

- Gather all candles, wax melts, holders, and accessories
- Check for scent strength, burn quality, and condition
- Toss crumbling, scentless, or unpleasant-smelling candles
- Clean candle jars and holders
- Group keepers by type or season
- Store extras neatly; display only a few at a time
- Donate unburned candles you won't use to shelters or donation centers
- Light a candle you love and enjoy the space you've made

🎁 One to Keep, One to Toss Challenge

Keep: The scent that instantly soothes you or makes your home feel magical.
Toss: The overpowering one that gives you flashbacks to a shopping mall perfume counter.

Week 39: Old Bedding, Spare Pillows & The Linen Pile That Ate the Cupboard

Bedding has a sneaky way of multiplying. You start with a sensible number of sheet sets… and then the spares arrive. The "guest" duvet cover. The extra pillows "just in case." The festive flannel set with snowflakes. Before long, you're playing cupboard Jenga with puffy duvets, flat pillows, and a mysterious fitted sheet that only fits a bed you no longer own.

I once pulled a pile down and found *five* pillow protectors and *zero* matching pillowcases. Also: one hot water bottle cover (no hot water bottle), and a duvet so thin I think it was just ambition sewn into fabric.

This week, we tame the bedding beast and make room for soft, functional, and fresh linen that doesn't threaten bodily harm every time you open the cupboard.

🎯 The Weekly Declutter Focus

Target Zone: Linen cupboards, under-bed storage, spare room closets—anywhere old bedding, duvets, pillows, and random linens hide.
Goal: Keep a clean, usable, reasonable number of

sheets, pillows, and blankets. Let go of the flat, the frayed, and the "what even is this size?"

Letting Go Tip + Memory Keeper Tip

Letting Go Tip: If it's stained, worn thin, smells like musty nostalgia, or no longer fits any bed you own—it's time. You are not obligated to keep the sheet set from your child's toddler bed just because it once featured dinosaurs.

Memory Keeper Tip: If one pillowcase or blanket carries real sentimental weight, clean and store it in your memory box—not stuffed behind five unmatched duvets.

Organising Advice

Pull everything out. Sort into piles: sheet sets, pillowcases, duvets, pillows, blankets. Match up sets. Discard anything torn, stained, smelly, or rarely used. Donate clean extras to shelters or pet rescues. Store sets inside one of the pillowcases for easy access. Use shelf dividers or bins for bulky items like duvets or seasonal bedding.

Pro tip: Two sheet sets per bed and two good pillows per sleeper is more than enough—especially if no one in the house is sleeping on a waterbed from 1992.

Decluttering for Empty Nesters

Mini Motivational Boost

Bedding should feel fresh, not frustrating. When you only keep what you use and love, changing the sheets stops being a dreaded task and starts feeling like an act of self-care. Plus, you'll finally be able to find a fitted sheet without swearing.

Checklist for the Week

- Pull all bedding and spare pillows from every storage area
- Sort by type and match full sheet sets
- Toss or donate worn, stained, or mismatched pieces
- Store sheets inside matching pillowcases
- Stack by bed size or room use (main, guest, etc.)
- Keep only what you use regularly—plus one seasonal set if needed
- Store bulky duvets or pillows in vacuum bags or clear bins
- Breathe in that clean linen scent with pride

One to Keep, One to Toss Challenge

Keep: A bedding set that fits perfectly, feels amazing, and makes your bed look inviting.
Toss: The flat, mystery-stained sheet that you've been "just using for the dog"—even the dog deserves better.

Week 40: That Box of Cords, Manuals & Warranty Papers for Appliances You Don't Own Anymore

There's always one. A shoebox, a drawer, a file folder labeled "Important," filled with booklets, paper warranties, and cords for devices that were possibly stolen by aliens or died in a puff of smoke years ago. You keep thinking, *I might need this someday.* Spoiler: you won't.

I once found a warranty for a vacuum cleaner we replaced in 2013, three identical USB cords (none of which fit anything I currently own), and a manual for a blender that exploded during lockdown banana bread season. Also: 24 twist ties and a battery charger with zero matching batteries.

This week, we pull the plug on outdated paperwork, mystery wires, and cord clutter—and restore order to your tech drawer (or at least *pretend* we know what half of it was for).

🎯 The Weekly Declutter Focus

Target Zone: Boxes, drawers, or folders of appliance manuals, receipts, random cords, and warranty papers.

Goal: Keep only what's still useful or relevant. Toss or recycle the rest without an ounce of guilt.

Letting Go Tip + Memory Keeper Tip

Letting Go Tip: If you no longer own the item, it's broken beyond repair, or you haven't used the cord in years—you don't need the manual, receipt, or charger. You really don't.

Memory Keeper Tip: If a manual reminds you of a major moment (your first big appliance, perhaps), take a photo of the front page for memory's sake—then let the paper go. The memory doesn't live in the cord.

Organising Advice

Empty the entire box or drawer. Group items: cords, manuals, warranties, receipts. Toss or recycle anything for appliances you no longer have. For current items, create a small folder or file labelled by category (e.g. Kitchen, Electronics, Outdoor). Label cords that stay and keep them in a pouch or cable organizer. And for the love of clarity—get rid of duplicates.

Pro tip: Most manuals are now online. Keep only what's truly necessary.

Mini Motivational Boost

Letting go of random cords and outdated papers is like deleting 3,000 mental tabs. Less "what if," more "I actually know what this belongs to." You're not just organizing—you're reclaiming brain space and drawer territory.

Checklist for the Week

- Pull out all cords, manuals, warranty booklets, and tech papers
- Recycle manuals for items you no longer own
- Discard expired or irrelevant warranty docs
- Match cords to current devices—label them clearly
- Toss duplicate or mystery cords you've never used
- Store remaining cords neatly in a bag or bin
- File manuals and warranties by category in a small folder
- Enjoy the bliss of one drawer that finally makes sense

🎁 One to Keep, One to Toss Challenge

Keep: A clearly labeled charger or manual for something you *actually* use.
Toss: The curled, yellowed warranty for a printer that lived its best life back in 2008.

Week 41: Decorative Lighting, Fairy Lights & Lamps You Forgot You Owned

Ah, decorative lighting. So twinkly. So whimsical. So... everywhere. One string of fairy lights turns into five tangled sets. Then you add that lava lamp from the early 2000s, the quirky bedside lamp shaped like a mushroom, and the string of solar lanterns that never charged properly but felt *festive* in theory.

I once opened a storage bin and found no fewer than seven strings of lights—three tangled, one half-lit, and one labeled "maybe works." Also: a lava lamp missing its lava and a Himalayan salt lamp that looked more like a potato. This week, we bring clarity (and literal light) to your glowing chaos.

◎ The Weekly Declutter Focus

Target Zone: Closets, attic boxes, drawers, or garage bins full of decorative lights, table lamps, broken bulbs, holiday glow, and solar experiments.
Goal: Keep lighting that works, looks good, and fits your current style. Let go of the dim, the dusty, and the doomed.

🗑 Letting Go Tip + Memory Keeper Tip

Letting Go Tip: If it's broken, flickers ominously, doesn't fit a single socket in your home, or smells slightly of "electrical risk"—out it goes. You're not running a haunted house.

Memory Keeper Tip: Got a light or lamp that's sentimental? Keep one meaningful item (like a kid's nightlight or the lamp from your first flat) in a memory box or repurpose it into something functional.

🧺 Organising Advice

Gather every light and lamp. Plug in and test them—yes, even that string of lights you've moved house with twice. Toss the broken, flickering, and frustrating ones. Sort keepers by use: everyday lighting, seasonal decor, mood lights. Wrap fairy lights neatly around cardboard or hang on hooks. Store extras in labeled bins, and keep current-use lights clean and accessible.

Pro tip: If a string of lights takes longer to untangle than it does to decorate—it's not worth the relationship strain.

💪 Mini Motivational Boost

Letting go of extra lights isn't dimming your joy—it's focusing it. You're choosing calm, clutter-free brightness over stress and dusty bulbs. Keep what lights you up. Literally.

Checklist for the Week

- Gather all lamps, strings of lights, and decorative bulbs
- Test each item to see if it works
- Toss or recycle anything broken or unreliable
- Donate working lights that no longer fit your style
- Wrap cords neatly and label seasonal or specialty lights
- Clean dusty lamps and bulbs
- Store neatly in bins or bags by category or occasion
- Celebrate by lighting your favorite lamp in a clutter-free corner

One to Keep, One to Toss Challenge

Keep: A beautiful, functional light that adds warmth or joy to your space.
Toss: The tangled strand of fairy lights with one sad, flickering bulb and a bad attitude.

Week 42: Magazines, Catalogues & Booklets You Swore You'd Read Someday

At some point, every magazine felt like a promise. "I'll read this with tea," you said. "Just a quick flip-through," you told yourself. And yet—there they are. Months (years?) of glossy covers stacked under coffee tables, on nightstands, and in that special "to read soon" basket that hasn't seen movement since 2019.

I once found a catalogue from a store that no longer exists and a parenting magazine with advice for toddlers. My toddler? Now a fully grown human who drives and pays taxes. This week, we let go of the pages of the past and reclaim those surfaces—and your sanity.

🎯 The Weekly Declutter Focus

Target Zone: Magazine stacks, bathroom baskets, nightstands, shelves, catalogue collections, and that ever-growing pile in the corner of the living room.
Goal: Keep only what you still *want* to read—and realistically *will*. Recycle the rest and free your flat surfaces at last.

🗑️ Letting Go Tip + Memory Keeper Tip

Letting Go Tip: If it's older than six months and hasn't been opened, it's time. You don't need to guilt-read every unread article about 10 ways to feng shui your spice rack.

Memory Keeper Tip: Found an article or photo that truly speaks to you? Tear it out and file it in a small "inspiration folder." That way, the whole issue doesn't become a permanent resident on your coffee table.

🧺 Organising Advice

Collect every magazine, catalogue, and booklet from every room (yes, even the bathroom). Create three piles: *Read Now*, *Recycle*, and *Inspiration*. If you want to keep one or two recent magazines for decor or reference—great! Otherwise, let go with love and a flick through first. Store inspiration tear-outs in a file or binder and keep one small tray or basket for your current reads—no more than three at a time.

Pro tip: Subscriptions can be paused or canceled. Digital issues count too—and don't take up table space.

Mini Motivational Boost

You're not failing because you didn't read that 2017 issue of *Real Simple*. You're evolving. Letting go of paper clutter is permission to live in the *now*, not the "maybe later."

Checklist for the Week

- Gather all magazines, catalogues, and booklets
- Flip through and pull out anything worth saving
- Recycle anything more than 6 months old you haven't read
- File favorite articles or inspiration in a slim folder
- Cancel or pause subscriptions you no longer enjoy
- Limit "current read" pile to 2–3 issues max
- Wipe down the surfaces your piles once buried
- Sit down with one fresh magazine and a cup of tea—guilt-free

One to Keep, One to Toss Challenge

Keep: A recent issue you're genuinely excited to flip through.
Toss: The 3-year-old catalogue for a home goods store that's already gone out of business.

Week 43: The Books You Keep but Will Never Read (or Re-read)

Books are beloved. Sacred, even. But sometimes… they're also dusty reminders of who we thought we'd be. That diet book from 2009. The 800-page epic you *tried* to get through (twice). The novel a friend swore you'd love. (You didn't.) And textbooks from courses you barely passed in 1998? Yep—still there.

I once found a book about kombucha-making. I've never made kombucha. I don't even like kombucha. I kept it for four years. Why? Because it *looked smart*. This week, we let go of shelf shame and make space for the stories, knowledge, and joy that actually fit who you are *now*.

◎ The Weekly Declutter Focus

Target Zone: Bookshelves, nightstands, coffee tables, boxes under the bed, and that weird stack of books propping up the printer.
Goal: Keep books that matter to you now—whether that's comfort reads, beautiful editions, reference material, or true favorites. Let go of the rest, guilt-free.

🗑 Letting Go Tip + Memory Keeper Tip

Letting Go Tip: If you didn't finish it, didn't like it, or have no real intention of reading it—release it. Books are meant to be read, not collected out of obligation.

Memory Keeper Tip: Love the inscription or memory tied to a book? Take a photo of the note inside, or save just that one sentimental volume and let the rest move on to new readers.

🧺 Organising Advice

Take all books off the shelf (yes, all). Sort into piles: *Love & Use*, *Read Someday*, *Nope*, and *Sentimental*. Be honest—if "someday" hasn't happened in 10 years, it might be a no. Donate unwanted books to local libraries, shelters, or Little Free Libraries. Organize keepers by genre, author, or color—whatever brings you joy. Make space for breathing room between the spines.

Pro tip: A shelf with space to grow is an invitation, not a failure. Your books are not your personality—just a reflection of it.

💪 Mini Motivational Boost

You're not betraying the written word by letting go of a book you won't read. You're honoring your time, energy, and space. You're making room for stories that excite you—not ones that sigh at you from across the room.

Checklist for the Week

- Take every book off the shelf or out of hiding spots
- Sort into: keep, maybe, donate, and sentimental
- Be honest about what you'll truly read or re-read
- Donate with joy—someone else will treasure what you didn't
- Dust shelves and wipe down book covers
- Re-shelve favorites by category, author, or color
- Leave breathing room for visual calm and new reads
- Treat yourself to reading one of your favorites in your new clutter-free nook

One to Keep, One to Toss Challenge

Keep: A book that made you laugh, cry, or see the world differently.
Toss: That trendy self-help tome you bought during a phase and never cracked open.

Week 44: Old Emails, Digital Subscriptions & Inbox Chaos

Your inbox was supposed to be a tool. A helper. A tidy, manageable communication station. But now? It's the Wild West of online newsletters, outdated promo codes, shipping notifications from 2017, and a haunting number of "just checking in" emails. And let's not even talk about the 17 streaming services you forgot you signed up for.

I once scrolled back and found an unopened email from 2014. The subject line was "URGENT." Well. It clearly wasn't. This week, we tidy your tech life and bring peace to your pixels.

🎯 The Weekly Declutter Focus

Target Zone: Email inboxes, digital subscriptions, newsletters, streaming services, and apps you haven't opened in months.
Goal: Reduce digital overwhelm. Unsubscribe, organize, delete, and simplify what's beeping at you for attention.

🗑 Letting Go Tip + Memory Keeper Tip

Letting Go Tip: If you haven't opened it in 3+ months, never signed up for it (hello, mystery mailing lists), or feel a small wave of dread every time it pings

—unsubscribe. You owe nobody your inbox real estate.

Memory Keeper Tip: Want to save a sweet email or important document? Create a "Digital Keepsake" folder and move it there. Let your inbox breathe.

🧺 Organising Advice

Start with a big sweep: archive or delete anything older than a year that's clearly irrelevant. Then unsubscribe from newsletters you no longer read (use a tool like Unroll.Me if needed). Create folders or labels for: Bills, Personal, Travel, Receipts, To Read. Sort recent emails into these folders. Finally, audit your streaming and app subscriptions—cancel the ones that no longer bring joy (or content).

Pro tip: Schedule a weekly 10-minute "inbox tidy-up" session from now on. It's like flossing—but for your brain.

💪 Mini Motivational Boost

A clear inbox = a clear mind. You're not just deleting emails—you're deleting distractions, guilt, and the constant "should probably check that." What stays now is what *matters*.

Checklist for the Week

- Delete or archive emails older than a year (or more!)
- Unsubscribe from unwanted newsletters and promo lists
- Create clear folders or tags for key email categories
- Move important or sentimental emails to "Keep" folders
- Audit and cancel digital subscriptions you don't use
- Delete unused apps or icons from your phone/tablet
- Turn off unnecessary notifications for less digital noise
- Enjoy a quiet inbox (even just for 5 minutes)

🎁 One to Keep, One to Toss Challenge

Keep: A personal or meaningful email that brings a smile.
Toss: That unread "Hot Sale Ending Soon!" promo from a shop you forgot existed.

Week 45: Craft Supply Chaos – Round 2 (Scrapbooking, Stickers & Ribbon Roulette)

Crafting is creative. Healing. Joyful. Until you've got 14 glue sticks, six sets of alphabet stickers, and ribbon so tangled it could serve as a plotline in a thriller. And then there's the washi tape. So much washi tape. You swear it breeds in the dark.

I once found stickers for a scrapbook theme I *never started*. "Family Beach Holiday 2012" — complete with sandcastle embellishments. We went to Wales. It rained. We didn't even make it to the beach. This week, we tidy the chaos and bring back the joy of creating without the avalanche of unused supplies.

🎯 The Weekly Declutter Focus

Target Zone: Craft drawers, scrapbooking bins, sticker folders, ribbon containers, and shelves of embellishments and dreams.
Goal: Keep only supplies that inspire creativity or are realistically usable. Let go of craft guilt and create a clutter-free creative space.

🗑 Letting Go Tip + Memory Keeper Tip

Letting Go Tip: If you bought it for a project you never started (or even remember), if it's dried out, broken, or just plain "meh"—let it go. You're not a craft supply museum curator.

Memory Keeper Tip: If something was part of a sentimental project (a finished scrapbook or a handmade gift), keep just one token item or take a photo. The memory is in the making, not in the clutter.

Organising Advice

Gather every craft supply into one space. Group by type: stickers, tape, stamps, embellishments, ribbon, scissors, adhesives. Discard duplicates, dried glue, crusty paint, or scraps "saved for later" (you won't). Use labeled bins, drawer inserts, or vertical trays. Hang ribbons on rods or dowels for easy access. Store your most-used items closest to your workspace.

Pro tip: A project box with *just* the supplies for your current craft keeps focus high and mess low.

💪 Mini Motivational Boost

Crafting should spark joy, not a stress response. By decluttering your supplies, you're clearing creative blockages and giving yourself permission to enjoy making—without digging through piles of past intentions.

Checklist for the Week

Decluttering for Empty Nesters

- Collect all craft, scrapbooking, and sticker supplies
- Sort by type: stickers, adhesives, ribbons, embellishments, etc.
- Toss dried, broken, or guilt-inducing items
- Donate good-quality extras to schools or community centers
- Use containers, dividers, or drawers to store by category
- Create a "Current Project" box for active use
- Label storage and make supplies easy to grab and return
- Craft something small and joyful with what you love most

🎁 One to Keep, One to Toss Challenge

Keep: That perfect set of stickers or ribbon that always makes you want to create.
Toss: The dried-out glitter glue and half-used embellishments that haven't seen daylight since the last Olympics.

Week 46: Clothes That Need Fixing or Altering (But Never Got There)

Every home has one: the Sad Little Stack™ of well-meant intentions. A buttonless blouse. Trousers that need hemming. That jacket with a broken zip that you *swear* you're going to repair (it's been four winters). Welcome to the section of your wardrobe that's not worn, not gone—just limbo.

I once found a pair of jeans I meant to patch... seven years ago. When I held them up, they had formed *natural* holes in places I didn't originally intend. They had evolved. This week, we face the fix-it pile and make peace with what stays—and what simply isn't worth the thread.

🎯 The Weekly Declutter Focus

Target Zone: The "fix or alter someday" pile—on a chair, shelf, bin, or haunting the back of your wardrobe.
Goal: Sort out what's worth mending, what's not, and either fix it, book it, or bin it.

🗑 Letting Go Tip + Memory Keeper Tip

Letting Go Tip: If it's been sitting for over a year, you forgot it needed fixing, or it doesn't even fit or suit you anymore—let it go. You are not legally obligated to rescue every broken zipper.

Memory Keeper Tip: If the garment is deeply sentimental (wedding guest dress, child's first handmade jumper), consider framing a piece of the fabric, making a keepsake from it, or storing it in your memory box with purpose.

🧺 Organising Advice

Lay out all the "to fix or alter" items. Sort into: *Quick Fix (under 15 minutes)*, *Needs Professional Help*, and *Let Go*. Do the easy ones right now—yes, *right now*. For the rest, set a date to take them to a tailor or seamstress (or don't, and be honest with yourself). Let go of items that aren't worth the time or cost.

Pro tip: If you wouldn't buy the item again today, it probably doesn't deserve the repair.

💪 Mini Motivational Boost

Letting go of the "fix me" pile doesn't mean you're lazy—it means you're real. Life's too short to trip over trousers you've been guilt-storing since 2015. You're allowed to dress in clothes that are already *ready* to wear.

Checklist for the Week

- Collect every item awaiting repair or alteration
- Sort by fixability: quick, pro help, or release
- Do quick repairs immediately (buttons, loose hems, etc.)
- Book a tailor appointment or call a sewing-savvy friend
- Let go of anything too far gone or no longer wanted
- Clear the chair, corner, or drawer that held the guilt pile
- Fold or hang finished items back in your wardrobe
- Celebrate by wearing something fixed—or letting something go guilt-free

🎁 One to Keep, One to Toss Challenge

Keep: A garment you still love that only needs a tiny tweak to wear again.

Toss: That top you meant to "turn into a cute crop" that's still shaped like disappointment.

Week 47: Suitcases, Travel Toiletries & the Never-Unpacked Bag

You swore you'd unpack right away. Just toss the laundry in the machine, put the toiletries back, and fold the suitcase neatly into storage. And then... life happened. So the travel bag stayed half-packed, the mini shampoo bottles multiplied like hotel rabbits, and now your toiletry bag has a crusty mystery cream and three expired plasters.

I once found Euros, sunburn lotion, and a melted lip balm... from a trip I took *pre-pandemic*. Also: a tangled necklace I apparently planned to wear with a beach dress that never left the suitcase. This week, we unpack once and for all—and prepare for future adventures without dragging the past behind you (literally).

🎯 The Weekly Declutter Focus

Target Zone: Suitcases, carry-ons, travel toiletry bags, pouches, adapters, passport wallets, and that backpack still holding travel socks from 2022.
Goal: Clear out old contents, toss the expired, and reset your travel gear so it's fresh, functional, and ready to roll.

🗑 Letting Go Tip + Memory Keeper Tip

Letting Go Tip: If it's crusty, expired, or was only used once at a hotel pool three countries ago—let it go. You don't need to hoard tiny toothpaste tubes like they're currency.

Memory Keeper Tip: Found a sweet little souvenir or ticket stub in your bag? Pop it in your memory box or travel journal. Not in the side pocket with the leaking conditioner.

🧺 Organising Advice

Empty every suitcase and travel bag completely. Toss expired products, old receipts, melted cosmetics, and duplicates. Wipe down toiletry bags and travel pouches. Group travel essentials: adapters, eye masks, earplugs, chargers, etc. Restock your toiletry kit only with travel-sized items that are current and actually work. Store everything in one labeled travel bin or suitcase so you're always ready to grab and go.

Pro tip: Keep your travel gear *empty but packed*—i.e., bag clean, stocked with the basics, but without random earrings, gum wrappers, and unidentifiable currency.

💪 Mini Motivational Boost

You don't need to carry the weight of old trips with you. Decluttering your travel gear is about clearing the path for new adventures—without the crusty SPF 30 from 2016 tagging along.

Checklist for the Week

- Gather all travel bags, cases, and toiletry kits
- Unpack anything still hiding in zippers or side pockets
- Toss expired items, mystery creams, and duplicate chargers
- Clean out toiletry bags and sanitize any containers
- Refill with fresh travel-sized essentials
- Group travel gear in one easy-to-grab area
- Store empty suitcases properly (nested or upright)
- Toss old luggage that's damaged, broken, or no longer functional

🎁 One to Keep, One to Toss Challenge

Keep: The travel pouch or toiletry case that's clean, compact, and easy to use.
Toss: The leaky, zip-jammed bag that smells like sunscreen and sadness.

Week 48: Childhood Keepsakes & School Projects You're Still Holding Onto

Every macaroni collage, paper mâché volcano, and "Mum, you're my best friend" scribble feels like gold. But decades later, those crayon masterpieces have turned into a heaving tub of yellowing paper, brittle art, and oddly sticky sculptures. You kept it all because it was adorable—and it was. But also: *how many spelling test papers from 1999 do we need*?

I once found a "Happy Father's Day" card… addressed to a pet fish. It was from 2005. No idea what the original plan was there, but I kept it for 18 years. This week, we sort the sentimental from the simply stored and curate a collection that actually fits in one box (and doesn't include glitter casualties).

🎯 The Weekly Declutter Focus

Target Zone: Plastic tubs, memory boxes, under-bed bins, closet shelves—wherever old art projects, report cards, and school photos live.
Goal: Keep the truly meaningful mementos and let go of the fading photocopies and forgotten worksheets.

🗑 Letting Go Tip + Memory Keeper Tip

Letting Go Tip: If it's crumbling, anonymous, duplicated, or just doesn't hold real emotional weight—it can go. You're not dishonoring your child's creative genius by tossing a finger painting they can't even remember making.

Memory Keeper Tip: Take photos of bulky or delicate items before letting them go. Create a digital keepsake folder or print a photo book with "The Best Of" school memories.

🎒 Organising Advice

Lay out everything and sort by child, age, or school year. Create piles: *Definitely Keep*, *Photograph & Recycle*, and *Let Go*. Keep one box per child with only the most meaningful items—art, awards, writing, or one item per year. Store in plastic document sleeves or acid-free folders. Add labels and a quick note about the memory if needed.

Pro tip: A curated memory box tells a clearer story than ten bins of forgotten finger paint.

💪 Mini Motivational Boost

You're not throwing away their childhood—you're honoring it with intention. When you keep only the treasures that still bring a smile or tear, you make room to actually *see* and enjoy them, instead of drowning in glitter dust and ancient glue sticks.

Checklist for the Week

o Gather all childhood art, school papers, and keepsakes
o Sort into: Keep, Photograph & Recycle, Let Go
o Take photos of bulky or fragile items before discarding
o Choose one box or folder per child for long-term storage
o Label items and group by age or year
o Recycle outdated or anonymous pieces
o Create a digital photo album if desired
o Store boxes in a dry, safe place where memories can breathe

 ## One to Keep, One to Toss Challenge

Keep: One meaningful, smile-inducing piece of art or writing that still melts your heart.
Toss: The 23 math worksheets from Year 4... unless they show early signs of Nobel Prize-winning genius.

Week 49: Ornaments, Decor & Trinkets You're Not Even Sure You Like Anymore

They came as gifts. Souvenirs. Random impulse buys during a phase where you "were totally into elephants." Now your home is peppered with dusty knickknacks that don't spark joy—just mild confusion and a lot of surfaces to dust.

I once found a decorative candle shaped like a stack of books with glitter flames. It was supposed to be "whimsical." It mostly just frightened the cat. This week, we declutter your decorative landscape so your home can breathe—and actually reflect *you*.

🎯 The Weekly Declutter Focus

Target Zone: Shelves, side tables, mantelpieces, window ledges, shadow boxes, and display cabinets—anywhere trinkets and treasures have made themselves at home.

Goal: Keep only the ornaments and décor that feel beautiful, meaningful, or truly yours. Let go of the dust catchers and decor fatigue.

🗑 Letting Go Tip + Memory Keeper Tip

Letting Go Tip: If you wouldn't buy it today, if it doesn't match your current style, or if you've secretly considered "accidentally" knocking it off the shelf—let it go.

Memory Keeper Tip: If something holds sentimental value, but not style value, take a photo or keep one beloved item from a collection and rehome the rest. It's the memory you love—not the mass.

🧺 Organising Advice

Clear one area at a time. Remove every item and give the surface a good wipe. Then ask, item by item: "Do I love this? Do I want to see this every day?" Curate small groupings if you like a styled look, or go minimalist and embrace open space. Donate what's in good shape—someone else might *actually* want a ceramic frog playing banjo.

Pro tip: Every item you let go of gives more visual peace to the ones that stay.

💪 Mini Motivational Boost

You are allowed to outgrow your décor. Letting go of an object doesn't mean letting go of the person who gave it to you, the place you bought it, or the season of life it belonged to. It just means your *current* self is taking the wheel.

✅ Checklist for the Week

- Walk through each room and gather all decorative knickknacks
- Ask yourself: "Would I buy this now?"
- Group similar items and choose your favourites
- Donate, gift, or recycle the rest
- Dust and clean shelves and surfaces
- Curate a few beautiful, intentional displays
- Store sentimental pieces if needed—but limit the stash
- Breathe in the calm of cleared, peaceful space

🎁 One to Keep, One to Toss Challenge

Keep: One piece that still makes you smile every time you walk by it.
Toss: The random travel souvenir that's been haunting your bookshelf since 2003.

Week 50: Holiday Decorations That Haven't Seen the Light Since the Last Ice Age

Holiday décor is equal parts magic and madness. It starts as a few baubles and lights, and somehow turns into 17 bins labeled *"Xmas Misc,"* a broken inflatable reindeer, and a tinsel garland that hasn't sparkled since the Spice Girls were topping charts.

I once opened a holiday box and found: a melted candle shaped like a turkey, a headless elf, and a "Happy New Millennium" banner. We are well past that. This week, we sort, prune, and preserve the cheer—without the chaos.

🎯 The Weekly Declutter Focus

Target Zone: Holiday bins, attic boxes, garage shelves, and under-bed décor storage.
Goal: Keep only the decorations you love, use, and enjoy. Let go of broken, outdated, or "why do I still own this?" seasonal clutter.

🗑 Letting Go Tip + Memory Keeper Tip

Letting Go Tip: If it's damaged beyond repair, hasn't been used in several years, or makes you sigh more than smile—it's time. Holiday cheer should not require an engineering degree or emotional negotiation.

Memory Keeper Tip: Keep one or two meaningful items from each holiday or tradition, and label them with a sticky note about their story. You're saving the *memory*, not the whole fake pine forest.

Organising Advice

Pull out *all* seasonal décor (yes, even the stuff that lives in "that one bin" all year). Group by holiday or theme: Christmas, Halloween, Easter, New Year's sparkle, etc. Test lights, glue loose bits, and toss broken or incomplete sets. Choose sturdy, labeled bins for storage, and use dividers or soft wrap for fragile items. Keep frequently-used items easily accessible.

Pro tip: If it takes longer to untangle it than it does to enjoy it… let it go.

Mini Motivational Boost

Letting go of excess holiday décor doesn't mean you're less festive—it means you're making space to enjoy the season without digging through guilt, glitter, or broken snow globes. Keep the traditions, not the tangled mess.

Checklist for the Week

- Gather all holiday décor from attic, closets, and bins
- Test lights and check condition of ornaments and décor
- Toss or recycle broken, faded, or sad-looking items
- Donate gently used decorations you no longer use
- Group by holiday and store in clearly labeled bins
- Use soft wrap or dividers for fragile items
- Keep only what you love, use, or plan to pass on
- Do a little happy dance—you just made every future holiday easier

🎁 One to Keep, One to Toss Challenge

Keep: A beloved decoration that brings back warm, happy memories every year.
Toss: The tangled string of lights that's been broken since the last ice age and still smells faintly of attic.

Week 51: The "Maybe" Box – Things You Couldn't Decide on (Until Now)

Every good decluttering journey comes with a "maybe" pile. The items that weren't obvious yeses or noes. The sentimental sock. The "useful someday" gadget. That slightly odd gift from your third cousin that you feel weird about giving away. So you tossed them all in a box and told yourself you'd come back with clarity.

It's been a year. The box has become furniture. I once found three scarves I forgot I owned, a cracked mug I'd emotionally outgrown, and a decorative plate that I think belonged to someone else's grandmother. This week, we open the vault and finally decide—with love, clarity, and zero guilt.

🎯 The Weekly Declutter Focus

Target Zone: The "Maybe" box (or drawer, bin, secret stash under the stairs) where uncertain items have been quietly gathering dust.
Goal: Make a final decision: keep, donate, repurpose, or release.

🗑️ Letting Go Tip + Memory Keeper Tip

Letting Go Tip: If you haven't needed, looked for, or even *missed* the item in the past 6–12 months, chances are, you don't actually want or need it. You were just buying yourself time. Good news: time's up!

Memory Keeper Tip: If something holds emotional value but isn't useful, consider photographing it or writing a note about its significance. Keep the memory, not the object.

🧺 Organising Advice

Lay everything out. One by one, ask: Do I love it? Do I use it? Would I buy it today? If not, let it go. Make quick, gut-based decisions. For borderline items, try the 10-second test: if you hesitate longer than that, it's probably a no. For anything you keep, find it a *real* home—no more "maybe" limbo.

Pro tip: Label this your **Final Decision Box**. No re-maybing allowed.

💪 Mini Motivational Boost

This is your decluttering victory lap. You've built the muscle. You've sharpened your instincts. You *can* decide. Letting go of uncertainty clears emotional clutter just as much as physical—and gives you confidence for future decisions.

✅ Checklist for the Week

- Find and open the "maybe" box, bin, or drawer
- Lay items out and sort by category
- Use the "love it, use it, would buy it" filter
- Toss or donate anything that no longer fits your life
- Photograph meaningful items before letting them go
- Find a proper home for anything you keep
- Recycle the actual "maybe" container—its job is done
- Celebrate your decisiveness with something small but satisfying

🎁 One to Keep, One to Toss Challenge

Keep: The item you rediscovered and realized you still *truly* love.
Toss: The object you forgot even existed—clearly, it's not essential.

Week 52: The One-Year Declutter Review & Letting Go Celebration

You started this journey with a sock drawer and a sense of chaos. 52 weeks later, you've tackled everything from broken fairy lights to forgotten family photos, crusty old travel tubes to emotionally confusing throw pillows. And through it all—you've laughed, let go, and found your floor again.

I once heard someone say, "Decluttering isn't about having less. It's about making room for more of what matters." After a year of decisions, nostalgia, dust, and occasional glitter explosions—you've done exactly that.

🎯 The Weekly Declutter Focus

Target Zone: Your whole home… but this time, with fresh eyes.
Goal: Reflect, revisit, and gently recheck areas. Celebrate your wins, tidy up loose ends, and recognize just how far you've come.

Letting Go Tip + Memory Keeper Tip

Letting Go Tip: Decluttering isn't a one-time act—it's a mindset. You're now equipped to let go of what no longer serves you as life evolves. This week, check for "clutter creep" in any areas and reset gently.

Memory Keeper Tip: Celebrate the memory-keepers you've intentionally chosen to preserve. Create a photo of your new memory box or journal a short note on how it feels to carry less—but remember more.

🧺 Organising Advice

Walk through your home slowly. Notice how it feels. Are there spaces that feel calm now? Others still tugging at you? Revisit any areas where clutter crept back (hello again, junk drawer). Reconnect with your systems. Refresh one or two key areas—not to start over, but to keep the momentum.

Pro tip: Create a short "Maintenance List" of monthly or seasonal tasks that will help you keep things clutter-free long-term. You don't need to redo the year—just revisit with intention.

💪 Mini Motivational Boost

You've transformed not just your home, but your mindset. You've proven that you can make decisions, hold memories without clinging to objects, and create space for the life you're living now—not just the one you used to have.

You didn't just declutter. You took your power back.

Checklist for the Week

o Take a walk-through of your home and notice any returning clutter
o Tidy up a few "re-cluttered" zones without guilt
o Reflect on what you've learned through this process
o Celebrate the areas that now feel peaceful, useful, or beautiful
o Create a simple plan for maintaining your decluttered space
o Journal a few notes about how you feel at the end of the year
o Treat yourself—yes, really! You earned this moment
o Tell someone you love about your journey and inspire them too

 One to Keep, One to Toss Challenge

Keep: One reminder of how far you've come—a journal entry, before/after photo, or meaningful object.
Toss: The guilt. The shame. The "shoulds." You don't need them in your next chapter.

You did it!

52 weeks. One whole-home transformation

Now it's time to live in your space—with room to dance, breathe, create, nap, and make new memories. The clutter is gone, but your story? It's just getting good.

Anissa Brodon

52-Week Decluttering Checklist

- Week 1: The Sock Drawer of Doom
- Week 2: The Kitchen Junk Drawer Jungle
- Week 3: The Mug Situation
- Week 4: The Coat Closet Time Capsule
- Week 5: Expired Pantry Party
- Week 6: The Mismatched Container Colony
- Week 7: The Toy Chest Time Forgot
- Week 8: The Dresser Drawers of Past Eras
- Week 9: The Glove Box Disaster
- Week 10: The Bathroom Product Parade
- Week 11: The Neglected Nightstand
- Week 12: The Shoe Shelf Shuffle
- Week 13: The Purse, Bag & Backpack Bonanza
- Week 14: Office Supplies, Pens & Paperclips Mayhem
- Week 15: The Magazine Rack Museum
- Week 16: The Scarf, Hat & Glove Avalanche
- Week 17: Forgotten Freezer Foods
- Week 18: The Tupperware Tower Tumble
- Week 19: Gardening Gear & Outdoor Clutter
- Week 20: The Pet Supplies Takeover
- Week 21: Car Boot Chaos
- Week 22: The Desk Drawer of Doom
- Week 23: The Filing Cabinet Fiasco
- Week 24: The DVD/CD Relic Shelf
- Week 25: Sentimental Clutter Part I – Cards, Letters, & Drawings
- Week 26: Sentimental Clutter Part II – Trinkets, Trophies & Tokens

- Week 27: The Mystery Cupboard You Haven't Opened Since 2011
- Week 28: The Linen Closet—Towels That Have Seen Too Much
- Week 29: The Filing Cabinet Full of Paper That's Not Even Yours
- Week 30: The Recipe Collection That Hasn't Seen an Oven Since 1999
- Week 31: The Gift Wrap Explosion
- Week 32: The Medicine Cabinet Mystery Tour
- Week 33: The Jewellery Box Time Forgot
- Week 34: That Drawer Full of Chargers, Cables, and Confusion (Yes, Another One)
- Week 35: The Pet Stuff Overflow Zone
- Week 36: That Drawer of Paper Bags, Plastic Bags, and Totes
- Week 37: The Perfume, Cologne, and Body Spray Graveyard
- Week 38: The Candle and Wax Melt Takeover
- Week 39: Old Bedding, Spare Pillows & The Linen Pile That Ate the Cupboard
- Week 40: That Box of Cords, Manuals & Warranty Papers for Appliances You Don't Own Anymore
- Week 41: Decorative Lighting, Fairy Lights & Lamps You Forgot You Owned
- Week 42: Magazines, Catalogues & Booklets You Swore You'd Read Someday
- Week 43: The Books You Keep but Will Never Read (or Re-read)
- Week 44: Old Emails, Digital Subscriptions & Inbox Chaos

- Week 45: Craft Supply Chaos – Round 2 (Scrapbooking, Stickers & Ribbon Roulette)
- Week 46: Clothes That Need Fixing or Altering (But Never Got There)
- Week 47: Suitcases, Travel Toiletries & the Never-Unpacked Bag
- Week 48: Childhood Keepsakes & School Projects You're Still Holding Onto
- Week 49: Ornaments, Decor & Trinkets You're Not Even Sure You Like Anymore
- Week 50: Holiday Decorations That Haven't Seen the Light Since the Last Ice Age
- Week 51: The "Maybe" Box – Things You Couldn't Decide on (Until Now)
- Week 52: The One-Year Declutter Review & Letting Go Celebration

Final Reflection Journal Page & Simple Maintenance Plan

Final Reflection Journal Page
1. How does your home feel now compared to when you started this journey?
2. What was the most satisfying space to declutter and why?
3. What surprised you the most about the process?
4. Which item was hardest to let go of—and how do you feel about it now?
5. What have you learned about your relationship with stuff?
6. How has decluttering affected your daily routines or mindset?
7. What are three things in your home now that bring you true joy?
8. If you could give one piece of advice to someone just starting this 52-week journey, what would it be?

Simple Maintenance Plan

Monthly Mini-Check (Choose one day each month):_____
- Walk through high-traffic areas (kitchen counters, entryways, etc.)
- Re-home anything out of place
- Clear one small drawer or surface that's collected clutter

📅 Seasonal Refresh (4x a year – Spring, Summer, Autumn, Winter):
- Revisit your wardrobe and linen closet
- Check for expired products in pantry/medicine cabinets
- Refresh seasonal décor and donate what you didn't use

🧠 Mindset Reminder:
- Ask yourself often: Do I love this? Do I use this? Would I buy it again?
- Keep a 'donate bag' somewhere visible so letting go is always an option

🎉 Celebrate Progress:
- Take a photo of your favorite clutter-free corner every few months
- Journal how it feels to live with more space and less stress

Decluttering for Empty Nesters

Index

Welcome to the Empty Nest	2
Week 1: The Sock Drawer of Doom	4
Week 2: Junk Drawer Jenga	7
Week 3: Tupperware—The Plastic Bermuda Triangle	10
Week 4: Where Old Chargers Go to Die	13
Week 5: Linen Closet of Forgotten Towels	16
Week 6: The Attack of the Expired Spices	19
Week 7: The "Just in Case" Cupboard (a.k.a. Doomsday Prep Lite)	22
Week 8: Under the Bed—A Dust Bunny Safari	25
Week 9: That One Drawer Full of Pens That Don't Work	28
Week 10: The Kids' Art Pile That Might Be Worth Millions (Emotionally)	31
Week 11: The Sentimental Shoe Graveyard	34
Week 12: The Coat Closet Black Hole	37
Week 13: Pantry Purgatory—Expired Goods & Ghost Snacks	40
Week 14: The Forgotten Luggage of Dreams	43
Week 15: Bookshelf Backlog—Are You Really Going to Read That?	46
Week 16: The Over-the-Fridge Mystery Cabinet	49
Week 17: Bath Products That Retired Before You Did	52
Week 18: Holiday Decorations That Should've Stayed in 1997	55
Week 19: The Craft Supply Explosion	58
Week 20: The Kids' Room Museum Exhibit	61
Week 21: Broken Electronics—Sentimental but Useless	64
Week 22: Old Phones and Their 78 Chargers	67
Week 23: The Sock Orphanage—Where Do Their Mates Go?	70
Week 24: Fridge Magnet Mania	73
Week 25: The Garage—Not Just for Regret and Cobwebs	76
Week 26: The Car Boot Full of Good Intentions	79
Week 27: The Mystery Cupboard You Haven't Opened Since 2011	82
Week 28: The Linen Closet—Towels That Have Seen Too Much	85
Week 29: The Filing Cabinet Full of Paper That's Not Even Yours	88
Week 30: The Recipe Collection That Hasn't Seen an Oven Since 1999	91
Week 31: The Gift Wrap Explosion	95
Week 32: The Medicine Cabinet Mystery Tour	98
Week 33: The Jewellery Box Time Forgot	101

Week 34: That Drawer Full of Chargers, Cables, and Confusion (Yes, Another One) 104
Week 35: The Pet Stuff Overflow Zone 107
Week 36: That Drawer of Paper Bags, Plastic Bags, and Totes 110
Week 37: The Perfume, Cologne, and Body Spray Graveyard 113
Week 38: The Candle and Wax Melt Takeover 116
Week 39: Old Bedding, Spare Pillows & The Linen Pile That Ate the Cupboard 119
Week 40: That Box of Cords, Manuals & Warranty Papers for Appliances You Don't Own Anymore 122
Week 41: Decorative Lighting, Fairy Lights & Lamps You Forgot You Owned 125
Week 42: Magazines, Catalogues & Booklets You Swore You'd Read Someday 128
Week 43: The Books You Keep but Will Never Read (or Re-read) 131
Week 44: Old Emails, Digital Subscriptions & Inbox Chaos 134
Week 45: Craft Supply Chaos – Round 2 (Scrapbooking, Stickers & Ribbon Roulette) 137
Week 46: Clothes That Need Fixing or Altering (But Never Got There) 140
Week 47: Suitcases, Travel Toiletries & the Never-Unpacked Bag 143
Week 48: Childhood Keepsakes & School Projects You're Still Holding Onto 146
Week 49: Ornaments, Decor & Trinkets You're Not Even Sure You Like Anymore 149
Week 50: Holiday Decorations That Haven't Seen the Light Since the Last Ice Age 152
Week 51: The "Maybe" Box – Things You Couldn't Decide on (Until Now) 155
Week 52: The One-Year Declutter Review & Letting Go Celebration 158
You did it! 161
52-Week Decluttering Checklist 162
Final Reflection Journal Page & Simple Maintenance Plan 165
Index 167